The Entrepreneur's Cookbook

Essential Measures for Business Success

The Entrepreneur's Cookbook

Essential Measures for Business Success

SHAZ NAWAZ

Urbane
BUSINESS

urbanepublications.com

First published in Great Britain in 2020 by Urbane Publications Ltd
Unit E3 The Premier Centre Abbey Park Romsey SO51 9DG
Copyright © Shaz Nawaz, 2020

A CIP catalogue record for this book is available from the British Library.

ISBN 978-1-912666-85-0
MOBI 978-1-912666-86-7

Design and Typeset by Michelle Morgan

Cover design by Michelle Morgan

Printed and bound by 4edge UK

urbanepublications.com

**THINK DIFFERENTLY ABOUT YOUR SMALL BUSINESS...
AND RADICALLY IMPROVE GROWTH, SUCCESS AND PROFITABILITY.**

CONTENTS

I want to tell you
how this book
came about.

In addition to running my own five businesses, over a period of years I conducted several thousand consultations with individual business owners and entrepreneurs, who came to see me because they wanted to achieve greater profit and growth. During these sessions I began to see a common and distinctive pattern emerge.

Almost all these business owners were asking me the same questions, experiencing the same difficulties and challenges, and making the same mistakes. And I was finding that there were specific strategies that I would be recommending time and again to help them achieve radically greater success. When my clients put these recommendations into practice, they worked.

These entrepreneurs and business owners wondered whether there was a book containing the solutions I was giving them. I could not find one, so decided to write it myself.

The Entrepreneur's Cookbook explains how to avoid the most common entrepreneurial mistakes, and details key practical actions to help you build a highly successful business. It is a survey of what to do and what not to do, providing a comprehensive framework of pointers to use in your business. These pointers work. A unique selection of real, practical tips and ideas which work day in, day out, for business owners and entrepreneurs everywhere.

Writing the book has been a rewarding journey for me in itself – gathering the material over a period of years, shaping it into a series of accessible segments, editing the content in more detail, and finding a publishing partner who appreciated what I was trying to do. I learned a lot more about business in the process!

I am particularly passionate about helping small business owners, but the book will also be of value to anyone in business, including CEOs of major companies.

I hope you find the contents helpful and that they prove useful in helping you positively transform your business. Dip into the sections that address the problems you are experiencing right now or are linked to the targets you want to achieve; or read the book from cover to cover. However you use the book you will find material to help you.

When aspects of your business evolve and develop, come back to the book again for the content that is most relevant to you at a particular time. I hope you will always find it a source of help and inspiration.

Shaz Nawaz

July 2020

Peterborough UK

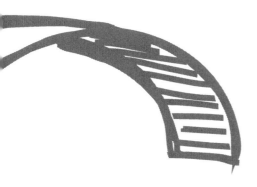

This book is dedicated to three groups of people:

1. To those who always believed in me and told me – even when I doubted myself – that I could achieve whatever I wanted.

2. To my team members – who go above and beyond every single day and are making a real difference to peoples' lives.

3. To small business owners – the real unsung heroes who are changing the world in their unique and special ways, often without even realising it, and with minimal fuss.

INTRODUCTION

In business, it is inevitable that we're going to make mistakes — that's part of the journey a business owner or entrepreneur takes.

Over the course of three thousand one-to-one consultations with business owners, I've found that everyone is keen to find out the mistakes that have been made by other business people - and by myself - in the hope they can simply avoid them. They want to know what went wrong, how it went wrong, and how they can stop it happening in their business. It's the smart thing to do – instead of making those mistakes yourself, you learn from others to the benefit of your own business and entrepreneurial plans.

Through my own experience of successfully advising businesses across a range of sectors and in a variety of industries, it has become clear there are several common mistakes which many business people make on their journey. Similarly, entrepreneurs want to develop a definitive list of priorities – the key 'dos' and 'don'ts' of running a business. Of course, there is no one thing, or three things, or five things ... success in business stems from an amalgam of many diverse elements which, when they are all brought together, make the crucial difference to overall results. At any one time, some of these elements will be more relevant to a business than at other times.

The success comes from recognising when to apply those diverse ingredients for the advantage of your business. The Entrepreneur's Cookbook examines and explains these key elements to provide a unique and comprehensive framework of actionable advice to use in your business. This is not simply a list of abstract principles, but a practical,

7

useable recipe for success, giving you the tried and tested ingredients required to drive massive improvement in your business.

There are plenty of 'gurus' offering abstract principles and strategies, many requiring experience to understand, let alone implement – that is not what this book is about. Instead I aim to provide real, practical tips and ideas which have worked day in, day out, for business owners and entrepreneurs across the world. And to show how, by changing your thinking, you can transform the growth, profitability and success of your business.

The time factor

We know business owners are busy, often spinning many plates at a time.

Time is a commodity no-one can get back; as you lose time, you lose money – and no business has an infinite amount of money it can invest indefinitely to get results. This book is designed to share resources that will help you maximise your leverage in terms of time and money and build results.

These resources have evolved very naturally over time from my many consultations with entrepreneurs and businesses. In essence, it is a valuable 'one-stop shop' of tools for every entrepreneur and business builder.

Who the book will help

The challenges faced by businesses are broadly the same whatever the size of the enterprise, it's just the magnitude of a problem that differs - and the solution too can be applied on a greater scale for a big corporate entity. A small business might have only five employees and could be encountering certain generic challenges of managing said workforce. A large corporation may have twenty thousand employees, but it will still face similar employment and management issues, just on a much bigger scale.

The principles for solving issues will also be basically the same; the rules for running a business are universal. If you look at any business of any size, it will have to face the challenge of cash flow; issues around operations; and tackle problems with publicity, marketing, HR or people management. These are all key areas for every growing business. These constantly recurring issues and solutions are covered in the main segment of this book.

The book is designed to suit entrepreneurs who have started their business journey but know they need help on a number of key issues – busy entrepreneurs who are ambitious and seriously committed to growing their business, but are facing challenges or have come unstuck in one area or another, and are looking for positive new ways of taking the business forward.

The book provides a resource that will resonate with any business owner who finds him or herself in this position, including CEOs of major companies.

How the book is arranged

I often make a gift of a book that I believe will be helpful to a business colleague or client. However, when I ask them six months later how they are getting on with the book, they almost always report they haven't started it. They look at a 400-page book and think "I just haven't got time to read this" – so they don't start.

This has dictated the rationale for the book's format. The main content is delivered in accessible, 'bite-size' chunks, each of which provide solutions to a specific business issue or problem area. Scan the contents, find the issue you want to tackle, read and digest the advice and suggestions, and immediately develop ideas for implementing positive actions relevant to the success of your business.

The book is designed to be a highly practical and useable resource to help you, the busy entrepreneur, as and when needed. There's no need to plough through pages of text – dive in and find what you need when you need it.

To further help you find the tips and solutions that are relevant to your needs, the content is generically collected into thematic groupings. If you just scan through these categories, you're sure to find one or two that will

immediately address a particular challenge you're facing right now.

I hope you will find the book both relevant and useful. Do please contact me if you'd like to share any feedback, or if you need solutions that go further than those you find here.

If you would like to **contact me:**

shaz@aa-accountants.co.uk

website **www.aa-accountants.co.uk**

Facebook page: **The Profits Wizard**

You Tube: **Shaz Nawaz**

Twitter: **@ShazNawaz1**

I'd be delighted to hear from you.

Now let's begin by assessing the six key phases of building and running a business, which will form a framework for the individual learning principles that follow.

UNDERSTANDING
THE SIX STAGES
OF A BUSINESS

This chapter identifies the six broad phases that businesses go through and highlights the principles you should pay attention to at each stage. These guiding principles are then set out in detail, with advice on how they are applicable across several phases.

An inordinately high percentage of businesses fail in the first few years of trading – as high as 90% - a number far too high to ignore. When starting a business, note that the odds are against you. You need to do everything you can to ensure your venture is in the 10% that survive.

Is this situation statistically due to bad luck, market conditions, bad choices of business sector, or poor decision making? I believe that it is often a combination of all four, but in my experience poor decision making is the most significant factor, and the one you can do something about. Therefore, it is important to think things through, consider carefully, and make the right choices, because those choices are going to define your business.

What follows are the six phases of the business journey.

Existing

Before you bring your business into existence, you need to do your market research; make sure that you're well prepared for the specific marketplace you're going into. Alongside that, have a strategic business plan that identifies key objectives and targets.

While doing your market research you should begin to spread the word about your business proposal. Speak to family members, friends, associates and former colleagues – anyone who is interested in talking to you about it. Talk it through with them, gauge their reaction and get their feedback. This is imperative; leave no stone unturned.

One of the key early decisions is setting the right price for your product or service. Focus on the margins in your business plan and in your projections. Start as you mean to go on by charging the right price from the outset, so that you can continue to have good margins as your business begins to expand.

Be very clear about your Unique Selling Proposition (USP); it should always present a sustainable competitive advantage. To help formulate this, ask yourself the following questions:

1

Why should someone do business with you rather than with any of your competitors? What's in it for customers if they buy from you? What need of theirs are you meeting? You need to be crystal clear on this before you launch your business.

2

What are the core values of your business? Being clear on these will serve you well as your business continues to exist and to expand. A core value is something you place at the centre of your business, representing what you are trying to do at the highest level. There are two broad interpretations of what is included in this term. Some people use it to refer to abstract qualities such as honesty or integrity or being open and transparent. To me, these are qualities anyone should aspire to anyway, and it's more helpful to think of core values in a more practical, specific and business oriented way.

Your core values, then, will be linked to your identity, to who you are, and to what your organisations stands for. They will inform and drive your business decisions. They will be affected by the type and scale of your business as well as by your personal values.

For an airline company, for instance, the core values might be to give passengers a better experience than a competitor can give, or it could be efficiency in getting passengers to their destination on time, or it might be dependability so that things like losing passengers' luggage don't happen. In the case of a more modestly sized business such as a web design agency, the values might focus on design, or could be about innovation and up-to-the-minute functionality. If you're self-employed or run a small business such as plumbing, your chosen core values might be about providing service with a personal touch, or focusing on trustworthiness.

3

Are you relying on hope and optimism rather than creating a solid business case? Hope is not a valid business strategy, so don't leave anything to chance. Make sure you have planned and prepared everything carefully and methodically.

Establishing

In terms of a start-up date, make sure you incorporate a good launch so that you can get the word out there. Your level of enthusiasm will, to a great extent, define your level of success. So be positive, go out and speak to as many people as you can through as many channels as possible.

The crucial point here is not to cut corners by taking on anyone and everyone as your first customers; this is the biggest mistake many businesses make on start-up. Securing the right customer is more important than securing any customer. Tread carefully; you have been warned. Be selective and discerning in this matter - in line with your business plan - and develop your ideal client profile.

It is also important in the establishing phase to set standards and then stick to them. People are often tempted to forego standards and quality in favour of speed and getting things done. But standards matter; people care about quality so make sure you maintain your standards in line with the values and USPs you identified in the 'existing' phase.

Many new start-ups go bust due to poor margins and bad cash flow, so learn from the mistakes of those who have gone bankrupt because of this. Your aim is to defy the high probability of failure by being in the 10% who succeed; you need to do things differently. Review your business plan regularly and make sure you are following it, because that is your #1 strategic document. Don't forget, you started your business to make a profit.

From the start, the key focus is on the customer and ensuring that you provide exceptional customer service; this will set you apart. Go above and beyond – be the best at this.

Finally, set your Key Performance Indicators and then track and measure them. A KPI is a piece of information or data that provides a crucial reflection of how a certain key aspect of your business is performing, enabling you to make better business decisions. KPIs for a large banking organisation, for instance, might chart the overall amount of lending happening at any given time, or the average customer feedback score, showing whether customers are happy. For an advertising agency, a KPI might be the number of new clients signed in the last month or the last year. With small businesses in general, important KPIs normally include net profit margins, or the amount of cash in the bank.

At this early stage, it's all about 'establishing' and not about 'scaling', so don't try to grow too quickly; never run before you can walk. It's important to lay solid foundations; growth will come later. Too many businesses try to grow too quickly and end up failing. Don't be like them.

Evolving

Now that you've established the business, the foremost concern should be to review your business plan, make sure it's still relevant, and update it accordingly. At the same time review your Key Performance Indicators (KPIs) and adjust them, if necessary, in line with your current plans.

If you haven't built up a habit of tracking your management information – the data and patterns which will tell you what to do and what not to do – then start doing so. Important data examples include sales, projected cash flow, customer growth, and relevant market trends such as those provided in Google Trends. The key data for you depends on what you're trying to achieve at any given moment. If you're looking for improvement in client retention, for example, you might track client satisfaction data in detail. If you're looking to increase your sales overall, then you will need to track your sales conversion rate, or the number of meetings with potential new clients.

Listen to the data and act accordingly. The data will drive your business. If you only respond at the end of the financial year it may be too late to effect necessary positive change.

Secondly, remain focused; focus is the key characteristic you must develop. Focus on yourself, on your business, on your customers, on your numbers and on everything around you. You want to **be proactive, not reactive.**

This could be a good stage to take someone on if you haven't done so already; but take your time to hire. Many businesses that run into staff difficulties have hired too quickly and hired in error. Make sure that the candidate is the right fit for your business, and that they have the skills and knowledge that will add to the profile and growth of the business. There's no point in hiring a mini-me! Then delegate; that will free you up so that you can focus on growing the business.

Don't become reliant on one big supplier, one big customer, one employee or one product. If you rely on just one supplier, for example, and that company stops supplying you, starts supplying your competitor, changes their business model so that they're no longer supplying what you need, suddenly start hiking up their prices, or goes bust, then you're going to have a major problem. Or if you're reliant on one main customer and that company decides to take their business elsewhere, the gap they're going to leave in your sales could be catastrophic. Relying on one customer, when they know it, can make you become beholden to them. They can dictate terms, push your prices down, or become demanding and make unreasonable requests. There are all kinds of things that can go wrong.

Furthermore, relying too much on one customer, supplier or product can mean inhibiting the development of diversity and flexibility in your offering – important qualities for a healthy and responsive business.

So, diversify. And now you can begin to think about growing your business.

Expanding

You may have several team members and a good customer base, so now is the time to start focusing on standardising systems and processes because they will help you expand the business. Furthermore, the business will not then rely solely on you. This is a weakness I've seen in many SMEs - when the boss/owner is not around, the business struggles.

You should also focus on developing a strong culture in which the company is living the values that were identified at the outset. **A values-based business grows better and quicker**. Your key members are in alignment, your customers are in alignment with you, you all have a shared sense of shared values that cement you together, create synergy and build relationships. It will help you attract like-minded customers who then spend more money with you and help you grow. It will help you attract like-minded team members, creating stronger teams where everyone is pulling in the same direction with a common sense of purpose.

Hire people with exceptional skills and, most importantly, make sure they have a good attitude. Essentially you are looking to hire people who will ultimately be better than you at the job you are employing them to do. Hiring like this is the true strength of a leader; it is not about ego, it's about what's best for the business.

Observe what is working well and repeat it. If you don't already have a marketing person or department, this is a good time to establish one. Create a marketing plan so that you're ready for expansion.

You may also want to consider securing a mentor – one who has been on the journey you've embarked upon, so that they can help and guide you. You can find a mentor by speaking to business colleagues and associates who have had previous experience of being mentored or have used a mentor they can recommend. You can also ask in any professional groups you belong to. Word-of-mouth recommendations where you receive feedback from someone you know, and trust, are generally better than more random methods such as web searches or social media sources that are unknown to you. Mentors have specialised experience and expertise, so find one who is familiar with and experienced in the issues you are facing or the skills you want to build. Have an initial meeting or chat before committing yourself, ensuring you've got the right fit. Be aware that there are countless individuals who have set themselves up as mentors or coaches but have never run a successful business in their lives.

Keep an eye on your costs. I often see small businesses trying to act like bigger ones – a potentially significant mistake. Live within your means and don't haemorrhage cash to feed a lavish lifestyle that you can't support. Lots of business owners struggle to live within their means. They might make £100k this year and anticipate a 30% growth for the following year – but then start spending as if they have that money now! Make the money first and spend it later. In the 'expand' phase, invest money in capital-appreciating assets such as property, stocks and shares or other types of business interests, rather than simply spending it all.

This is also a good time to consider whether you should 'niche'; or look at vertical opportunities, including different products, services or markets. Becoming a specialist within your marketplace is one way to grow a business quickly. It means you get better at what your producing and what you're selling and become more widely known for it. This is covered in detail in the segment on niching.

Exponential growth

By now you should have established strong foundations, so it is time to build on them. The focus should be on growing your profits and not your turnover; too many business owners destroy their business by concentrating on high turnover and compromising their margins to achieve it. Not a good idea.

Remember:

Turnover is vanity, profit is sanity, cash is reality.

This will always be valid.

Because you're now looking to scale your business, look at different markets and office locations; but don't be careless – you want to grow in a strategic manner.

Something else that works exceptionally well in this phase is looking at joint venture opportunities; this is a good way to grow exponentially. Look, for instance, at how Costa developed a joint venture with Esso, BP with Mace stores, and Disney with ABC and ESPN. Small or medium enterprises can benefit from this too at their own scale.

Consider joining a mastermind-type group with like-minded people. When looking to grow quickly there are certain traits or abilities you will need, such as coping with a higher level of risk, growing teams, taking on more debt, and working at a faster rate. This can lead to more

mistakes, so being part of a group, whose members have been through these experiences, can help you reduce errors, solve problems and get to your goals quicker.

Also take a look at multi-channel marketing, whether online or offline. Contrary to what some professionals believe or hope for, there is no single marketing channel that will enable a business to grow above all others. Yet many businesses become overly reliant on one particular channel such as Facebook or LinkedIn or Google, or perhaps favour direct mail or print media. Your clients are in different places and work in different ways, so you need to be flexible to connect with them. **Grow your net of marketing** so that you're capturing leads from a variety of sources.

Innovation may be appropriate in tech businesses, but in most fields, it may be best to rely on the methods that are tried, tested and trusted. Do not spend money on innovation if you don't need to or get carried away with it for its own sake. Innovation is one of those shiny-object-syndrome items that people can spend a lot of money on. Avoid taking silly risks; you made it this far and you don't want to screw it up now. "If in doubt, leave it out" is my policy – go back to your data, see what it tells you and stick with it.

Add more layers to your offering. Think about what else your customers buy that you could sell, because the hardest challenge for every business is securing new customers.

Now that you've got them, they trust you and you want to find ways to monetise that.

Also think about leverage, which is all about duplication and multiplication: in terms of your staff, your customers, your marketing, your distribution channels and even your suppliers. Focus more on what you are doing as a business, because that's what you control, and pay less attention to the competition. I find that too many businesses are paranoid about what other people in their sector are doing. It's good to be aware, but spend more time, energy and focus on your own business.

Whatever you do, don't get into a price war if you're not a really big company. A price war is often a race to the bottom, and everybody loses. Your margins will suffer – and business is always a game of margins.

Another really important point in this phase is to avoid focusing on sequential or step-by-step processes; that's not how exponential growth works. Focus on progressing aspects of the business simultaneously: that's how mature businesses grow quickly.

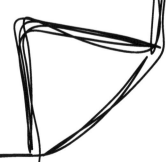

Finally, focus on the **'PESTLE'** influences on the business:

- Political
- Economic
- Social
- Technical
- Legal
- Environmental

Keep an eye on all these factors, watching out for any developments that offer opportunities to exploit.

Endurance and Exit

It is important at this stage to streamline all your operations and consolidate what you have.

If you're beginning to consider exiting your business but are undecided, think about equity - not about income – and the things you can do to build that equity. When considering the possibility of exiting, there are three broad options:

1

Sustain what you have – but it's unlikely that you're going to sustain if you already have a growth model.

2

Keep growing – this is more likely to work because you have already become an established business.

3

Exit.

Remember, most entrepreneurs make their really big money when they exit the business and not while they are running it. If you're looking to sell there are several options:

* You could offer a management buy-out to your staff or team.

* You could pursue a partial sale.

* You could push for an all-out sale.

* Or if you want to stay on in the business but don't want to spend so much time there, you could step back and offer shares to key personnel.

If you are looking to sell, you've done the hard work and now is the time to enjoy the rewards – and well done for remaining in the 10% and not the 90%!

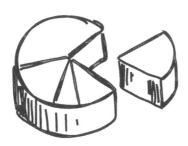

Changing Your Thinking

Here is a simple demonstration of how fixed thinking can be a limitation for your business:

An elephant can lift over one tonne with its trunk: it's one of the most powerful animals in the world. But in many images of working elephants or even vintage posters of circuses, you often see the elephant standing quietly, tethered by a thin rope to a small post in the ground. The elephant could quite easily break away, so why doesn't it?

It is because when the elephant was young and small it was tethered with a heavy chain, and no matter how hard it pulled it could not break free. It soon comes to accept that it cannot break free from this tethering. No matter how big and strong the elephant grows, it continues to believe that it cannot break free when tethered to a post. If only the elephant could change its thinking, it would understand its true power and use it.

I have found that entrepreneurs often fall into the same trap. They start thinking like that elephant of old. They have the potential to be immensely powerful, but are limited by long-held habits, beliefs and biases. There can be a strong tendency to continue doing things the way you've always done them. But if you change your attitude you can broaden your horizon and discover other possibilities.

Our thinking is the basis of everything we do in business, but a lot of people aren't taking the time to stop and analyse their thinking – they're too busy doing. It's simpler and more comfortable to keep doing what you've been doing rather than changing, learning and adapting, critically analysing and questioning why you've been doing something in a particular way. For example, a business might continue to focus on one category of customer, even if that customer base is in decline. Or fail to update its internal systems – potentially saving on overheads and improving efficiency – because 'we've always done it like this'.

I'm not advocating adapting every aspect of your business for the sake of it. But there are clear benefits to consistently taking the time away from the doing to focus on thinking about the key facets of your business.

Much of this book highlights individual aspects of your business where you might change your thinking and reap rich rewards.

Now let's look in detail at how to progress successfully through all six business stages, one aspect at a time.

CHAPTER 2

KEY THINKING
ON STRATEGY
& BUSINESS
DIRECTION

CASE STUDY

Bill Thompson was running a cash-and-carry business, offering wholesale and distribution of food products. He had an annual turnover of £1.5m, but even with staff support he was working longer and longer hours, day and night, and becoming increasingly stressed. Things were getting worse year on year, with the business struggling to grow. The stress was evident in Bill's personal health and in his family life – what there was of it, with the hours he was working. Bill just kept hoping things would get better, but they didn't. He wanted different outcomes, but he wasn't making any changes so things kept going in the same direction: downwards. He began to wonder if there was any point in carrying on the business.

At last Bill got advice and decided to instigate a thorough review and assessment of the business. The first thing he realised was that he had no clear vision for it, so he went back to basics and thought about why he had started the business in the first place, what he wanted to get out of it and what was important to him now, with a view to getting clarity on these points before doing anything else.

Bill decided that his aims – for himself and for his customers – were to have a thriving business, to offer excellent customer service, to create an environment for his team members in which they could grow, develop and thrive, and to have quality time with his family.

Now that Bill was clear on what the business was about, he immediately set about looking at the practical changes he could make. Already he was going to work with a spring in his step, as he had done years ago when he started the business. It felt like he was starting afresh with new enthusiasm and vigour.

Bill went back to the strategic drawing board, looking for ways to change the business model in order to meet the objectives he had identified. Looking at the overall picture, the first point he identified for change was that he had been unsuccessfully endeavouring to supply everything to everybody, a comprehensive wholesaler of convenience and a supplier to one and all. He took a long hard look at his customer base in order to identify the type of customer that was most profitable for his business – and which he most enjoyed offering his service to. It quickly transpired that there were clear groups fulfilling these criteria. Of these, supplying restaurants and takeaways was the clear leader, but ice cream suppliers also stood out.

Bill then set about making changes focusing all his efforts on serving these niche markets. He had previously worked in a takeaway, so knew that industry well. He decided to prioritise supply of quality products, and to develop his branding by creating a new line packaged under his own name, selecting products which he knew would work well for the restaurant trade. This produced an immediate increase in sales.

Secondly, Bill identified that he had always looked towards his competitors in order to make his own decisions on pricing, product range and marketing; he realised that he had been fixated on whatever the competition was doing. This also meant he had always assumed he could only generate a certain level of profit margin.

Bill now decided that it would make sense to keep an eye on what the competition were up to, but not necessarily follow them slavishly - or even be overly influenced by industry norms. He began to experiment with testing and tweaking things, charging different margins for different product groups, particularly in light of the increased demand within the market niches he was now focusing on. It quickly became clear which of these increases were viable and could be made permanent or increased further. This measure produced a dramatic improvement in turnover and profit. He was now reaching many more clients.

The success of these first measures - and the fast growth they produced - greatly increased Bill's confidence. With his improved margins he was able to invest more in staff, sales and targeted marketing, and in additional strategies which supported further rapid growth. Over the next couple of years, the business's turnover doubled, and in subsequent years it increased by 30% annually.

Another piece of breakthrough thinking on Bill's part involved a large carpark which was part of his property. In earlier years this had been full of customer vehicles - but Bill was now delivering to many of his bigger customers so most of the carpark was empty and unused. Bill hit on the idea of buying empty industrial storage units to place there, and offering storage rental deals to his best customers, most of whom wanted to buy in greater bulk but did not have sufficient storage space of their own. The dramatic increase in sales revolutionised Bill's figures and attracted further new customers who had small premises with storage issues. As Bill purchased the containers outright, all additional income from this source was pure profit.

Bill now reflected on the fact that much of his new success had come in ways he could not have expected, that it had been necessary to step outside the daily running of the business to look at new possibilities. His turnover increased from £1.5m to £10m during this period.

From originally working 70 to 80 hours a week, Bill was now delegating a great deal to highly motivated staff and efficient operating systems - and working 20 to 25 hours weekly. Bill's health and home life improved dramatically.

THE RECIPES

2.1: NO POINT IN RUNNING TOWARDS NOTHING

Key results you will gain from this section:

◊ ***Learn how to generate a clear vision for your business development.***

◊ ***Define your objectives clearly.***

◊ ***As a result, gain benefits such as knowing what steps to take next and alignment of your teams.***

Before doing anything, you need to be crystal clear about your business goals, the purpose your business serves and the direction you're planning to take.

In your business, you need to set a very clear vision for:

A) the outcomes you want to move towards, and

B) what your business will look like at a certain point in the future.

You will also need a clearly defined mission. Some people see this as their purpose, others call it their **'Why?'** – in other words, why are you in business? You'd be surprised how many start-ups have not considered this question fully.

If you don't have these clearly defined goals, and a clear sense of what purpose you're trying to achieve, then you won't know where you're heading. And if you don't know where you're heading then you won't know when you've arrived – or how to get there!

Types of directional decision

Let me give you some examples.

A company might set a goal of increasing turnover by £1m in the next 24 months. Having decided on the figure, they can then break it down into smaller quarterly or monthly targets, and also decide what individual departments or staff will each need to achieve to meet the overall aim. Everyone then knows what their individual target is and what their priorities should be.

Another company might decide "We want to become the biggest supplier of our product/ service in the region." For instance, "We're going to be the biggest supplier of vacuum cleaners in eastern England/ West Wisconsin/ Uttar Pradesh/ Central Mongolia." In order to achieve that, what key objectives need to be identified? Once those objectives

are confirmed, the business can make further decisions, such as increasing turnover to a certain level, opening new outlets in the region, or developing a more effective online platform.

You always need to have clear numbers and clear parameters for what you want to achieve. Vagueness and muddling along just will not do. A goal or direction is actionable, lack of direction isn't - you're just running towards nothing.

There are broadly two such types of goal or directional objective:

1) Tangible goals like turnover, profit, money in the bank, number of customers and so on.

2) Softer goals like "We want to be known as offering the best service," or "I want a better work/life balance."

Benefits of having a clearly defined objective:

- Gives a cue for what steps to take to move towards what you want, rather than just taking random un-thought-through steps – or no steps at all.

- Gives focus and aligns you and your team with key major objectives and sub-objectives, so that you know what is important at any given time and are unified with everyone pulling in the same direction.

The mistake of not having clear direction

Lots of people in business have a degree of clarity about what they're broadly hoping to achieve in order to be successful, but don't work out the detail of what they want their business to look like in the future. All they know is that they vaguely want to be successful. They neglect to define what that success looks like, or what is of most importance, or what needs to be done in order to achieve that success.

Many businesses 'plod along' and sincerely do the best they can, but they don't have much of a plan. And if you don't have a plan of your own, then you'll usually find that somebody else will make a plan for you – your team members, your customers, or your competitors – and their actions will determine your future.

For instance, let's say you're a business owner who has no clearly defined direction for the company. You will probably be leaving your team members to their own devices, saying in effect "You manage this particular area," or "You manage this growth aspect of our business." People in this position aren't best placed to know how to grow the overall business, so they are likely to plod along too, or say "our target will be to achieve 'X' outcome." But with some analysis, you as business owner might be more interested in achieving outcome 'Y', leading to a conflict of interest within the business itself.

Without clear direction and focus, you're going down a particular path thinking you'll achieve the broad objective you have in mind, but you're taking a route which may well be deviating from what you really want. Ultimately, after two or three or five years, you could be in a place which is totally at a tangent to where you wanted to be. It's like travelling without a map, compass, satnav or co-ordinates to a destination. The business has been running towards nothing.

This must apply to anything you do within the business. If you don't know where the end destination is and what it looks like, then it's highly unlikely that you'll get anywhere near it – or worse, become utterly lost on the journey.

If in doubt

Here are some helpful pointers. If you're not clear on what your direction should be, then ask yourself the following questions:

QUICK TIPS ✓

- Why are you in business?

- Why did you start your business?

- What was driving your enthusiasm?

- What do you want the legacy of your business to be?

- What do you want your business to be known for?

- What do you want your business to do for you in terms of return on investment? Is it more money, or is it something else such as more time, employing people meaningfully, or something else again?

Your answers to such questions will provide clarity on basic aspects of identifying a direction and objectives – and what the business should look like when you've achieved them.

Action points

* Think through and write down: why you started your business, or why you are starting it now; what your priorities are in creating the business; what you want to gain from the business; and where you would like it to be in five years' time and ten years' time.

* Apply these principles as you build your business, or apply changes based on them if your business is already up and running.

✳   Remember these principles and continue to apply them as your business develops.

✳   Periodically review the business, to check whether you are maintaining the priorities you set out at the beginning.

✳   It is possible that you may wish to change some of your priorities as progress unfolds. In which case, create a formally revised set of priorities, rather than just letting the original version slip, or having no priorities at all.

2.2: IT'S NEVER TOO LATE TO MAKE A START

Key ingredients you will gain from this section:

◊   *stop regretting what's happened in the past.*

◊   *learn from people who have failed and gone on to greater success.*

◊   *Identify actions for moving forward.*

No matter what you have done or what has happened up to now, you can still make a successful start.

The crucial thing for every entrepreneur and business to recognise is where they are in terms of positioning and performance, and that they are there for particular reasons.

People often spend too much time comparing their situations with that of others – usually those performing well. This can create feelings of inadequacy or failure. They wish that they could turn back the hands of time and make a new start. That, of course, is not possible; but what we can do is make a start today to ensure that we create a better business.

It is never too late. As a business person or entrepreneur, it's very important to realise that the beauty of being in business is that we can always make up for lost time. Think about it: many bankrupts go on to achieve great success. The reason they can is because the lessons learned from bankruptcy helped them better understand their capabilities, their situation, and how business works. This creates the building blocks for future success. Examples of bankrupted business people who have gone on to greater success include Henry J. Heinz, Hilary Devey, Walt Disney, Barbara Corcoran, and – yes – Donald Trump.

By looking at the behaviour of bankrupts who have gone on to recover and be successful, we can do the same. If we're at a place in our business where we're not happy, then in a way we're one step ahead of others because we now know what we *don't* want. Knowing what you want is important,

but it's equally important to know what you don't want.

Procrastinating and focusing on feeling upset with yourself means that a huge opportunity is being wasted: you're sitting there doing nothing and time is going by. It is vital to take action, to learn, revise and adjust; this will help you achieve far better results. For example, Silicon Valley tech companies are said to prefer employing people who have experienced failure.

Don't ponder all your life. As Nike say, © Just do it!

Action points

✳ Take action now rather than procrastinating.

✳ Whatever happened in the past is a source of learning for what you do next.

✳ Learn from people who have failed in the past and gone on to great success.

✳ Don't spend time comparing yourself unfavourably with others.

2.3: NICHING

Key results you will gain from this section:

◊   *Explore the potential benefits of niching.*

◊   *Look at how other businesses have effectively used niching.*

◊   *Think about how niching can apply to your business.*

Finding and developing your business's natural niche can be a hugely beneficial and profitable way forward.

From working with a significant number of client companies and individuals, I've realised that business specialists earn twice as much as business generalists - if not three times as much. My experience tells me that this correlates with higher rates of general success and career satisfaction too.

So whenever possible, I advise going deeper into a specialist area as opposed to going wider and being a little bit of an expert in a lot of different areas. I call this ***niching***.

When you become a provider of niche services or products, you tend to know a lot about one particular area. You become known for a specialism, can build a focused customer base, and ultimately charge more for your specialised offering.

Let me give you some well-known examples. KFC are known for selling chicken, Subway are known for selling sandwiches. They don't spread themselves too far beyond these specialisations. Parker produce high quality pens. The Financial Times focuses on financial information. Bang & Olufsen are leaders in high-end audio.

The same can be seen in the service sector. In the field of accounting, there are general accountants who will prepare non-specialist accounts and do your tax returns. Then there are specialist accountants who only work in one such area such as personal tax, business tax, VAT, tax investigation or property tax.

In the legal sector, there are general practices and practitioners who will do your conveyancing, buying or selling your house, writing wills, maybe matrimonial and even some criminal law. Then there are specialist legal firms – firms that have established a reputation for litigation skills in one very specific area. These are the highest fee earners.

In medicine, you find specialists like brain surgeons or heart surgeons, or those who specialise in handling emergency cases at A&E. Of course, there are also General Practitioners in medicine, and they perform a vital service – but they don't earn anywhere near as much as surgeons or consultants. They are the epitome of generalists; they know a little about a lot, rather than a lot about a little.

There are vast numbers of business consultants and business coaches worldwide. Many of these are very generalised, but there are also consultants who niche – for example, in helping you exit your business, leveraging the value of that business, and helping you sell it. And there are life coaches who specialise in helping you become a writer or finding your career direction. The services of these coaches, if they are expert in their field, are surely going to be more highly valued than someone who helps across the board.

The Mistake of Not Niching

The mistake or missed opportunity of being too generalist, then, is that:

QUICK TIPS ✓

1. You are not known for any one product line or service.

2. Too many people are generalists, so it's a noisy marketplace where it's extremely difficult to stand out or differentiate yourself and your product or service.

3. It is very competitive in price terms, so it's difficult to justify charging more than others for what you offer.

Once you niche, not only do you develop skill in that area, you can then leverage that skill further by writing articles, blogs and books, and become known as an authority. Then you become the 'go-to' expert. Once that happens, more people come to you, and you can charge a premium price for your service or product, because it's perceived to be of higher value than a generalised offering. To be seen as a specialist can be very rewarding, to be recognised as an expert in a specific field or fields. This also creates an 'enjoyment factor' - the pleasure of not only doing a good job but knowing you are perceived as an expert.

If you're a generalist and you spread yourself too broadly, people will unfortunately tend to think that you lack expertise in many areas. They may well be wrong in that assessment, but that's what they will tend to think. That's the nature of the customer's mind.

Furthermore, in any marketplace there will always be more generalists than specialists. As a specialist there are less people like you, so there will be more demand for your service or product – and because there is more demand and less supply, you will be more highly valued, and you can charge more for it.

It will also be easier for customers to find you, because of the specific nature of what you're offering and the smaller number of competitors – especially in this age of internet searching (provided your website and data is effective!).

You will also have more clarity than a generalist on exactly who your ideal customer or client is, and where to find him or her.

Action points

❋ Have a look at your business offering and think about how making it more niche could help you grow.

❋ Look at your current client base and see if you have a sizeable number of customers in one area – make that your niche.

❋ Ensure your niche is a sector where clients are able to pay high fees – it must be a profitable niche.

❋ Ensure clients have a growth mindset in that niche.

❋ Make sure you are passionate about that sector/area.

❋ Always continue to research the sector, keeping abreast of developments and becoming ever more expert.

❋ Learn the language of the niche – each sector has different words and phrases which you must know in order to be part of the inner-circle.

2.4: COMPETITION: GOOD, BAD – OR BOTH?

Key results you will gain from this section:

◊   *Don't see competition as all bad.*

◊   *Distinguish between helpful and counter-productive competition.*

◊   *Learn how to respond to what your competitors are doing.*

Competition may be more favourable for your business than you think; but a key decision is when to follow what competing businesses are doing, and when to do something very different.

It's of central importance to make progress in your business, but experience shows that on your own the potential for progress can be limited. Often, when competing with others to achieve an objective, we strive harder in order to succeed. We all know this from our own lives; we may well have experienced it in a sports day or other contest which we entered as a child, excelling in the face of other competitors. Certainly, in my role as a city councillor I've long observed that for a local or national government to make good progress and perform ever better, it benefits from strong opposition. The same principle applies equally in the world of business.

Of course, it is tempting to think the optimum position would be to exist as the only product or service provider in the marketplace. If you or your business don't have any competition, surely success is guaranteed? But think about a company like Nike; would they really be as good as they are without the competition from Adidas and Reebok? Would Mercedes make cars as well as they do without BMW and Audi breathing down their necks, pushing them to think differently and come up with innovative solutions and technological developments?

A converse illustration of the same principle can be seen in what happened in 2019 to Thomas Cook, and previously with companies such as Maplin and Toys "R" Us. These firms were unable to keep pace with the competition and embrace the changes their competitors were making - primarily moving a significant part of the business online. Inevitably the competitors secured market share. Now these three companies are a thing of the past, extinct species in the inexorable process of business evolution.

Competition keeps you on your toes; it forces you to think harder, to think differently, and to come up with better strategies. We should always see competition as healthy and embrace it.

It's important, then, to be aware of your competition: to know who your main competitors are, and what they're up to. Do not, however, be tempted to always blindly copy what they are doing. If you see them doing something smart, then look into that and consider how you can adopt, adapt and improve on it for your own needs. But don't spend precious time and resources fixated on your competition's every move. You can't control what they do; you can only control how you react and plan. You don't want to always be on the back foot, trying to second-guess what your competitors are doing and mimicking their developments. Many businesses and entrepreneurs make this precise mistake; they're so fixated on the competition they lose focus on what they need to be doing, based on the bigger picture. In fact, there is often an argument for observing what the majority are doing, discerning their predominant direction, and then going in the opposite direction.

As an entrepreneur you must distinguish yourself from your competition. You need to have a very clear and unique selling proposition, to ensure that there is something distinctly different about your offering and what you stand for, so that customers will choose you above everyone else. You need to stand out from the rest. Examples of companies that stand out in their crowded marketplace include Netflix, Pret A Manger, EasyJet and Purplebricks online estate agency.

In other words, you have to see what the marketplace is calling for, and then offer that in your own distinctively different way.

Action points:

* See competition as healthy and embrace it.

* Know who your main competitors are, and what they're doing.

* Only imitate what your competition is doing if it's a smart – and profitable – move for your company.

* Don't be fixated on your competitors' every move.

* Find clear ways of distinguishing yourself and your offering from the competition.

2.5: GROWING YOUR BUSINESS

Key results you will gain from this section:

◊ *Understand how business growth works.*

◊ *Discover different ways of achieving growth.*

◊ *Decide which methods are best for you and your business.*

Business growth is one of the key outcomes you should seek. There are many ways you can go about it.

As the owner of your business, you should spend significant time on growth and how to achieve it. What are the different ways you can grow your business?

1. Get the pricing right for maximum profit.

2. Secure more customer leads and make sure you convert a greater number to actual sales.

3. Ensure your existing customers buy more from you.

4. Ensure existing customers buy from you more often.

5. Reduce the attrition rate at which you are losing customers; ensure customers stay with you longer, perhaps by improving customer service.

6. Buy stock more affordably and find suitable ways to reduce your overheads.

7. Systematise everything so that you become more efficient and effective.

These are the seven ways to grow a business; focus on all of these areas because small incremental improvements in each of them when combined will exponentially equate to significant overall growth. Here's an example of how this works:

Effect of small incremental improvements:		
	NUMBERS AT PRESENT	IMPROVEMENT
Number of customers at start	250	
Sales leads	50	55
Conversion	50%	55%
No of customers	250	258
Average price	£250	£255
Average amount bought	2	2.2
Frequency	2	2.2
Total sales	£250,000	£318,424
Direct costs (10%)	£25,000	£31,842
Fixed costs	£150,000	£150,000
TOTAL PROFIT	£75,000	£136,582

Of these seven principles, getting the price right is the quickest way to build growth and profit. Keep an eye on your key performance indicators (KPIs). These include:

Topline numbers	Turnover
	Number of customers
	Profit
	Bank balance
Sales drivers	Number of leads
	Number of prospects
	Sales meetings
	Conversion rate
	New customers
	Average value of customers
Cost drivers	Direct costs
	Marketing costs
	Staff costs
	Overall debt
	Debt w/off
	Fixed costs
Success drivers	Number of complaints
	Team ideas
	Team training hours
	Number of testimonials
	Customer delight score
	Customer retention

As well as KPIs, you should also focus on:

- Key result areas. These are the areas of your business that you particularly want to grow, such as turnover, profit, or perhaps marketing.

- Income generating tasks, such as additional marketing or training team members.

Other components in the business can be delegated, but all the growth aspects listed above must be your own responsibility if you are to secure growth. Also consider:

QUICK TIPS

- Focus on how you can take your business from being ordinary to being extraordinary.

- Challenge the industry norms; this will transform your business.

- Focus on process. Process helps with transparency, so that every team member knows what they must do. It helps with efficiency, stops duplication, and supports integration of diverse functions within the business. It mitigates risk and makes the business less people-dependent and more valuable as a result. We all have processes in our businesses even though we may not recognise them as such. Identify your processes, fix the ones that aren't

working, and further improve those that are. Having no processes means that your business is relying wholly on you and therefore has no market value and cannot survive without you. If you don't know where to start with processes, begin by looking at the core components of the business such as sales, marketing, operations and so on.

- Don't forget why you're in business. Don't worry about criticism. Be congruent with yourself.

- Track numbers, and benchmark yourself against others in your industry. Ferociously measure everything. Make sure there is accountability. Pay attention to detail, as that's where businesses most often fall short, particularly as they grow. And make sure you improve overall standards in your business – high standards equal high performance.

- Finally, diversification is another way of growing your business.

Action points

✳   Use the classic core principles of business growth: correct pricing; more customer leads; ensuring customers buy more, more often; and that they stay with you longer.

✳   Systematise every process you can.

✳   Assess growth progress with key performance indicators.

✳   Diversify.

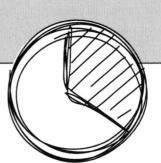

2.6: BREAKTHROUGH THINKING

Key results you will gain from this section:

◊ *How breakthrough thinking can help.*

◊ *How others have achieved it.*

◊ *Strategies to become better at it.*

Reliably making breakthroughs is not an accident; it is all about getting into the habit of thinking differently.

The world is changing constantly, and the way you perceive and think about the world needs to change constantly too.

The essence of needing a breakthrough implies that you're stuck, limited, or not making progress, that you have a problem you've tried to solve repeatedly but failed, or tried to make a particular change and it hasn't happened. Something radical is required to break through that limitation or that restriction.

Let's look at examples of major breakthrough thinking. Apple under Steve Jobs, of course, did this all the time; Jobs was constantly pressing his teams to make very specific and demanding breakthroughs, to order. He did this with iTunes, transforming how people listened to and acquired music; in a market used to buying CDs, Apple made it downloadable online. He came up with the concept of the smartphone, taking the phone far beyond simply making calls. He then extended this thinking to the iPad.

Steve Jobs wasn't simply thinking "What do people want?" (though there is an essence of 'want' in the way Apple trade on their products being desirable). He was thinking, "What do people really need, that they don't yet know they need?" - breakthrough thinking. Allegedly Henry Ford did likewise; if he had asked people what they wanted they would have asked him for a faster horse. Instead he gave them a car - breakthrough thinking. The telephone was considered a poor idea when it was first invented. People thought personal computers would never catch on. Ryanair and EasyJet broke through in the travel market with cheap airlines. Online shopping was a huge breakthrough. So was the smart TV.

In order to make a breakthrough, you need to think differently to how you have been thinking to date – you have to be open to thinking in a novel way, looking at things with a different perspective, coming from a radically different place. This doesn't mean you won't succeed if you don't produce or offer an entirely breakthrough product or service; but you need to apply breakthrough thinking at opportune moments in the development of your business offering.

If I'm looking for a way to overcome a particular challenge, or take advantage of an opportunity, rather than thinking of just one solution, I always think of ten ways of achieving that particular result. One way of dealing with things usually doesn't turn out to be sufficient, and very often is not the best solution. Listing ten or more ways of approaching the situation helps you think about which is genuinely going to be the best; and thinking up more solutions than the immediately obvious one prompts your creative thinking, moving you positively towards a solution that will represent a genuine and influential breakthrough. Proceeding in this way also affords the opportunity to amalgamate one or two different approaches to create a new and more radically effective solution.

To help with your creative thinking, ensure you take time away from the office/workplace. Being in a different setting away from the everyday business can help open your mind up to more ideas.

It also makes sense to look at the approaches in fields and markets other than your own. I often look at businesses which are different from mine, especially when I'm travelling or in leisure time. If I go to a restaurant, shop or shopping centre and see innovative, positive products or services, I find myself thinking about how I can apply them in my own businesses.

One such example which has led me to adapt ideas for my own business situation has been Disney, whose resorts I've visited on holiday with my family. Disney started off by making movies and then a theme park; but then went on to build theme parks targeted at children and featuring Mickey Mouse and other key characters. However, in order for kids to have fun, parents have to have fun too, otherwise the family is not going to come back. Disney developed activities for grown-ups too. Then they thought: if people want to come here repeatedly on holiday, how about we offer them time-share properties so that they can invest in real estate in the world of Disney. They even started offering Disney weddings – a wedding at Disney World in Florida costs $100,000 or more. There are also cruises, and they even offer booking for events and conferences at Disney World. And so on. The Mouse has done pretty well so far!

It was all breakthrough thinking. They were constantly thinking, if a customer is willing to pay for X, what else (Y and Z) can we sell them? Disney also considered the concept of payment. Customers don't like using cash, or even physically paying by credit card – it means carrying something additional around the resort/s. Disney created a secure wristband which the customer can purchase for a small fee – this is then connected directly to the customer's credit card. When they go shopping or undertake any chargeable activity, they just swipe their wristband – no need to reach into their pocket, wallet or purse to find money or pull out a card, they just use the wristband.

This has worked well and is extremely popular. No doubt customers with wristbands spend more than those without – and have more time to spend on spending!

Similarly guests don't need to carry purchases around with them. If they are staying at a Disney hotel, they just give a shop employee their room number and the goods are dropped off at their room. People are unimpeded by having to carry goods around with them, which would otherwise be a limiting factor. As Walt Disney said, "I hope we never lose sight of one thing; it was all started by a mouse." And look at what that mouse has achieved.

It is this type of breakthrough thinking that can inspire fellow entrepreneurs and businesses. A question I ask myself, that helps me look at things in a different way, is this: If anything were possible – absolutely anything at all – how would I run my business? Particularly if there were no restrictions on time, money, or staff. Another thing I use as an analogy is this: If I want to make an extra £50k in my business next year, I begin by considering what it would take to make £1m more. I write down every single aspect I would have to consider and implement in order to make a million pounds. That list is obviously going to be longer than it would be for making £50k. Then I think: Okay, from all these actions that are going to make me a million pounds, how many can I ACTUALLY DO in the next year? If I aim for those, and do as many as I can, then I can be confident that I can achieve an additional £50k in revenue – if not more. And usually it's more.

We often create limitations when we say to ourselves, "I need an extra £50k; what should I do?" So I say, move away from that thinking and aspire to a much bigger target. Even though your real target might still be £50k, consider it as ten or twenty times greater, which will make your thinking bigger, more creative and more radical.

If you need £50k for instance, you should look as widely as possible at all the things you could do to raise that money: get a loan from a family member, friend or bank; sell part of the business; sell some of your assets; employ an additional sales person; use existing staff to develop sales; or look at how you can reduce your expenses or your overheads. So rather than focusing on just one thing to get to where you want to be, examine and list *all* things you could possibly do to get the result you want. One idea is never enough, because coming up with just one idea and stopping there never achieves breakthrough thinking, it is too limiting. Applying that one single first idea usually falls short of your expectations.

Action points

* Look at how major entrepreneurs have made world-changing breakthroughs.

* Open-mindedly consider many potential solutions to a problem, then go with the one that brings a radically different approach.

* Take a break or change your location in order to get a different perspective on the business and your priorities.

* Come up with variations on what you are already doing to create new business opportunities.

* Aim high - be radical!

2.7: SUCCESS IS WHERE YOU LEAST EXPECT IT

Key results you will gain from this section:

◊ *Why some people seem to find success easier than others.*

◊ *Strategies for success thinking.*

◊ *How being adventurous supports achieving success.*

Clues to success can be found in unexpected places; it's important to pay very close attention and always be looking for those clues.

My experience is that those who are not doing well in their business are usually not paying much attention to what's going on around them. They stick to what they know or what they think is going to work, and fail to learn, even from ideas that didn't work previously. Running a business is about continuously gaining new insights, knowledge and experience which you can apply profitably.

To be successful, you need to be strategic in your thinking. You need to try different ideas, and new variations on existing ideas, to see which works best – because nobody knows which idea is going to work optimally in practice. But this needs to be applied within a strategic methodology. Most people in business have their habitual blind spots and are routinely missing opportunities that could drive success.

I say to people all the time: "You can't read the label when you are inside the bottle." By this I mean that people often don't see the bigger picture, because they're so 'in it'. They need to come out of it and look at all aspects of their business with a bird's-eye view. If you're knee-deep in what you're doing, you will often miss the obvious. Success is found – not always, but usually – in the really simple, obvious areas.

A common pattern which I often come across, as an aspect of being successful or otherwise, is when business owners try to second-guess their clients. They make assumptions with regard to what clients are going to buy or not buy from them, how much they are going to be prepared to pay, and which clients are going to be good customers/clients and which ones aren't. More often than not, I get these things wrong; most of my business clients admit that they get them wrong too. If we get that wrong, what else are we going to get wrong? We have to stop this habit of 'assumption', and instead have a mindset where we aim to keep testing possibilities. Some of these possibilities are going to work and others are not. The aim is to find successful patterns and correlations, and from these derive the most effective ways forward: which actions to keep, which to change, and which to drop.

Here's an example from my own business. When I started my accounting practice, we were typical tax-compliance accountants, aka 'bean counters'. Then I developed a strategy for widening the value offered by the business through adding coaching services. In my own mind, I did not expect this to be a successful strategy; I worried that people were not going to be interested – why would they want to pay an accountant for consultant advisory services? I was against it in my own mind. But I had the courage to test out the idea, and it turned out to be the biggest single win in the history of the practice, helping me to completely transform the business.

The big benefit was that each single client could potentially become the equivalent of two. Those customers who were previously only buying accountancy services could now also buy coaching. We had created two revenue streams from the same clientele, and that additional revenue hadn't generated any additional cost through marketing or sales activities. The new services also attracted new clients who had not been using our accounting services. There was another benefit, too. Accountants are generally seen as a necessary evil, but by offering coaching services we were helping clients grow their business, increase their profits, improve their cash flow, or think about exit planning

– and all this was adding extra value. Our clients were happier with us, and would stay with us longer, improving retention rates and bringing a lot more referrals through clients pleased with the range and scale of benefits they were getting. Finally, clients were willing to pay more for an extended set of services because they are adding value to their own businesses.

Had I allowed my initial scepticism to win out we would never have tested the proposition. Be bold and brave, have the courage to test different ideas.

Bear in mind also that where you least expect to find success is where others will least be expecting to find it too; so there will be fewer other people going in that same direction as you. This means that if you are courageous enough you could be the innovator, the ground-breaker, one of the first to do it. You will have a clear competitive advantage and be ahead of the pack. This is extremely important for a small business in particular.

All business owners should be searching for new challenges and looking at things through a different lens; that is how and when new opportunities will be discerned. This may mean that you also need to have around you other people who can give you that new perspective and ask you questions that you may not be asking yourself.

Action points

✱   Don't just do what you've always done. Try out different approaches and see what works.

✱   Think strategically. Take a bird's-eye view of your situation and potential.

✱   Don't be afraid to do something different from your competitors in the marketplace.

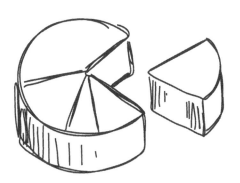

KEY THINKING ON CUSTOMERS AND MARKETING

CASE STUDY

Fred Lancaster was a building contractor working on all types of building contracts, from home extensions and building individual houses, to repairs and renovations to commercial offices, including some work for small property developers.

Fred found he was perpetually running round like a headless chicken, yet the business wasn't doing particularly well. He felt like he was racing all the time, just to maintain the same level of success.

His first critical step to improving the scope of the business was to try to work out which of his different customer types worked best for him and start to focus on working more for them and less on the others. He quickly realised that the customers he most enjoyed working for – and who were also the most profitable – were the small developers for whom he would build one to fifteen dwellings. The way he described this to himself was that these projects were "much more meaty" and "much less bitty" – the 'bittiness' was what had him running round in circles and making less money.

These developer contracts were indeed much more profitable because of the scale of the operations and the repetition they involved. He could buy supplies for them in greater bulk, enter into contracts with the suppliers, and get credit for them, all of which meant lower costs.

Focusing more on this work, Fred was building an excellent reputation for working well with developers, and so found he could charge more than he had been. He built up good contacts with architects, planning consultants, quantity surveyors and council officers, which led to more such work. His knowledge of planning and related matters enabled him to help developers who had run into difficulties and introduce them to others who could help. He found he was also able to help his clients sell their properties off-plan, including to housing associations that might purchase the whole development. He was clearly bringing added value to developers in the way he handled their building contracts.

Fred now found he could also more accurately target the individuals who made buying decisions among these modest-scale developers. He identified his ideal client as generally male and between 40 and 55 years of age. This was the sort of person he could personally relate to. He knew their demographic and he could accurately adjust his marketing to match this particular type of lead. He found that Facebook was particularly useful, and he joined a local chamber of commerce networking group which had a sector for developers, resulting in a stream of good leads and then contracts. He also carried out research into this category of developers in his region and ran a closely targeted and highly effective direct mail campaign to reach them.

The results of all these measures were impressive. Turnover rose from £1.4m at the beginning of the overall campaign to £3.2m today – and the profit part of this figure increased too. Most importantly, he wasn't running round like a headless chicken anymore.

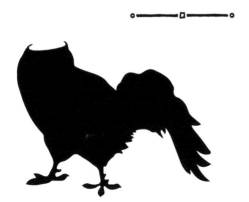

THE RECIPES

3.1: KNOWING YOUR IDEAL CUSTOMER

Key results you will gain from this section:

◊ *Discover the single worst thing you can do when it comes to customers.*

◊ *How to build an 'ideal customer' profile.*

◊ *Using this profile profitably for your business.*

Building a detailed profile of your ideal customer or client is absolutely crucial to business success.

When I ask business people "Who is your customer?" the most common answer I get is along the lines of "Everyone with a pulse!" That is the worst possible answer. Rolls Royce don't target everyone. Bang & Olufsen don't target everyone. Primark don't target everyone. Even Aldi and Lidl don't target everyone. They all know their target customer.

You have to be absolutely clear about who your ideal or optimal customer is. In order to do that, you need to focus on two things:

QUICK TIPS

- Demographics: your customer's age, gender, background, education, income, where they live, and so on.

- Psychographics: how they think, what they read, what are their fears, their biggest challenges, what keeps them awake at night, their worst nightmare, their aspirations, their dreams, their ambitions, what they secretly desire.

When you are creating a profile of your optimal customer, ask yourself all these questions. There are two situations in which you can apply this approach, and each can be employed as an ongoing process.

Where there are existing customers, look at your customer base and segment it through these criteria. Then look for the common trends in that customer base and break down the customers into groups such as A to C or gold/silver/bronze according to their value to you. The best customers are those who stay the longest, spend the most with you, and are most profitable, so these will rank highest.

For a new business, or where new clients are comprehensively being sought, sit down before taking any marketing action – or ideally before you've launched your product or service – and think about who in particular it's going to be for, and who will most benefit from it. If starting from scratch, you could run focus groups to explore which of the criteria listed apply to your potential best clients, and what demographic and psychographic profile points best fit with them. Alternatively, you could start with a blank sheet of paper or spreadsheet, and think about who you want to target, bearing in mind all the different attributes mentioned above.

If you don't have clarity on who this optimal client is, then you may fall into the trap of thinking that everybody is your customer; and if you think that, then nobody is. Be very clear on who your ideal customers are.

By building up a profile, you will be able to connect with your target customers and talk to them directly. They will then see that you 'get' them, that you understand their business and motivations. It is important that you learn the language that these particular people speak.

If you're targeting a specific industry sector, it will have a particular language, vocabulary and jargon. Property developers, for instance, use acronyms like GDV (gross development value), IPR (internal rate of return), ROCE (return on capital employed), plus other frequently used terms such as permitted development, conditions of planning permission and so on. If you can confidently use the language of the community you're targeting, you can connect better with them, they will trust you more easily, and they will see you as one of theirs.

For all these reasons, and as mentioned previously, I would strongly recommend that you develop a niche. If you have a niche, then you can focus on particular clients and know them better, thereby securing more customers, and charging more because you will be perceived as having more relevant experience and expertise. In addition, your reputation and profile will grow more quickly in that sector. It will be easier for you to be considered an expert in that field. For more detail on niching, see section 3.3.

Once clear on your ideal customer profile, then need to focus on where you can find these customers. For example, you might find that your ideal client is into classic cars; then you can advertise or market yourself wherever classic car aficionados are, including their events, magazines, and social media. Or your ideal clients might be into horse riding and you go where they gather. So now instead of fishing in an ocean where the fish are hard to find, you're fishing in a pond, so you're likely to catch more fish.

Stop thinking that anyone and everyone is your ideal client. Think about who that ideal client really is, then research everything about them – and most importantly, how to reach them.

If you're struggling to identify your ideal customer, look at the existing customer base, and in particular the top 10% of your customers (who generally speaking will be generating 80% of your profit). Think about what characteristics and similarities they share, then target more individuals and more groups who share those characteristics. You can then also refine your offering to better meet these needs and desires. If you find you really can't identify any pattern in your best customer profiles, then think about how your product or service can be made more specific so that you're targeting a particular type of customer.

Action points

∗   Do **not** believe that everyone can be your customer.

∗   Build a detailed profile of every aspect of your ideal customer: their demographics and their psychographics.

∗   Learn how your ideal customer talks and communicates and use the same language to connect with them.

∗   Work out where your ideal customer is to be found and connect with them there.

3.2: GENERATING LEADS

Key results you will gain from this section:

◊ *Different ways of generating leads.*

◊ *How to work out which of these ways you should use.*

◊ *The single most powerful and cost-efficient method.*

There is no point in marketing and advertising other than to generate more customer leads. This should be the only marketing aim for a small or medium business owner.

With marketing, I see so many smaller businesses copying large corporates, forgetting that they don't have the same budget or the same aims for their business. Large corporates are in the business of brand building. They want to be seen and talked about everywhere: on TV, on billboards, in print media, on the radio, on buses, in underground tube stations and of course online. Visibility is key for them and they can have ten figure budgets to achieve this. Coca Cola, for instance, spent $3.5 billion on advertising in 2018; that's the economy of a modestly sized nation.

Small business owners may think they have to do something similar because there must be a good reason the corporates do it. But small enterprises are not primarily in the business of building a brand – they're all about securing more customers. This is why lead generation should be your key focus.

There are many different ways to generate new leads and it makes sense to use as many as you can (within the limits of your budget), trying out a full range of methods so that you can identify which ones work best for your set-up and offering. Here are some examples:

- Networking

- Social media advertising, primarily Facebook, Twitter and Instagram

- Ad words, primarily Google Ads

- Direct mail

- Email campaigns

- TV or radio

- Print advertising

- Referrals

Of these, referrals from existing customers, suppliers and other contacts is by far the best and the most effective; also, the quickest and most cost effective.

You need to work out the lifetime value (LTV) of a client: how long they are going to stay with you on average and how much money they are going to spend with you in that time. Once you know that LTV, work out how much more it will be worth spending to generate such leads. For instance if you have a client who spends £2k annually with you and remains a customer for four years on average, then the total customer LTV is £8k. Ask yourself how much you are willing to pay to generate leads in order to find a new customer worth that. This will be your cost per lead. Once you've worked that out, you need to outspend your competition in order to move new leads from them to yourself.

The cost per lead is one of the biggest costs for a small business; we are always spending money to try to get more clients. It's a cost, but it's also an investment because it's going to deliver our biggest asset: the customer base. This is generally not seen on the balance sheet, but don't scrimp by trying to spend less money on securing clients. Nearly everybody else out there is trying to cut corners; you want to be the opposite and work out the maximum amount you can afford to spend on generating more, profitable leads.

If you have a product for which a lot of customers pay a small amount - which would produce a low client LTV - then you could consider ways to upsell, perhaps by adding complimentary products or services. If you sell them more, they have become more valuable customers.

Once you are clear on what you can spend on cost per customer, you can then apportion how much of that budget you want to spend on each form of lead generation. It would be nice if there was a simple equation to work this out for all businesses, but the reality is that you have to base this on your particular criteria such as your margins, the clientele you're targeting, and how aggressively you want to grow. We're talking here about precise spending through precise marketing channels and knowing exactly what that customer is worth: this is key. For example, if a potential new customer is worth £500 to you in lifetime value, then you should be willing to spend a very different amount on attracting them, compared to another customer who is worth £100. It might be worthwhile spending £100 on acquiring the £500 client, but only £10 on the £100 customer.

Whenever you do any kind of lead generation activity, I suggest you include the following elements in your content:

QUICK TIPS

1. Make sure you have an irresistible offer people cannot refuse. You cannot afford to engage in a lead generation activity which doesn't contain a definite offer. I see companies paying lots of money all the time for a nice brochure or advert that looks great but contains no clear offer. How will people receiving it know how to respond, or even know whether they want to respond?

2. Make sure you have testimonials. No matter how many times you tell someone how good you are they're not going to believe you. But if another customer tells them how good you are, they're more likely to believe it. This is why online sites like TrustPilot, Google reviews and TripAdvisor are so important and popular. The more positive reviews a restaurant has on TripAdvisor, the more likely a new diner is to go there for the first time. So ensure you have testimonials.

3. Make sure you have a unique selling proposition (USP).

4. Have a guarantee.

5. Always lead with a strong, clear headline at the top or front of the communication to capture people's attention, as newspapers do.

6. Include a deadline that customers should respond by.

7. Put a bonus offer in there too, to further encourage people to respond if they are sitting on the fence.

8. Make sure you have great copy. Don't be tempted to write it yourself if you don't have copywriting skills.

Remember, you're in the business of getting customers. Make that your #1 mission. And be clear on your #1 customer profile.

Action points

* Be very clear what kind of customer you want to be a viable lead for you.

* Use a variety of methods for generating leads and find out which work best.

* Using referrals is the single most powerful and cost-efficient method you can use.

* Work out the value to you of a lead, and from that work out how much you can spend to generate each new lead.

* Make sure each lead-generating activity includes a clear offer.

3.3: TARGETING PROFITABLE CLIENTS

Key results you will gain from this section:

◊ *Why it's advantageous to target high paying clients.*

◊ *Where to find more profitable clients.*

◊ *Additional measures you need to take with high paying clients.*

Targeting a limited number of customers with higher spending power is generally more achievable than targeting a much larger base of clients with smaller budgets.

Obviously, there are certain companies that do well by targeting a broad customer base that may not necessarily be cash rich – for example Walmart or Primark. But remember that if you sell 'em cheap, you have to stack 'em high, and sell your products in vastly greater numbers. One of the most straightforward ways for the rest of us to increase turnover and profit is to go for customers who are willing to pay a higher price for your particular service or product, thus giving you a bigger margin. In general, these are going to be customers who can afford to pay more. With a more modest customer base you can still do good business as long as you get the margins right.

The key measure is to offer a better quality of product or service commensurate with higher prices. This way you can do less work but make it more profitable. There is an old saying in business that pricing low is often a race to the bottom, so it makes sense to target customers who are willing to pay higher prices for the right product or service.

It can be a good strategy to focus your marketing on people with spending power, not those with smaller budgets. It's the same amount of effort either way, so why not put that effort into gaining customers who are going to constitute a more valuable asset? Because let's not forget, customers are your most valuable asset. They may not appear on your balance sheet, but they're still your biggest asset.

In order to engage successfully with affluent clients, you need to know a lot about your customers. As noted in the previous section, you have to know where they are; you have to know what they want; you have to get to know their language and how they talk so that you can connect with them.

Of course, ensuring you have customers with good cashflow also means they pose fewer problems when it comes to getting paid. They are least affected and last affected by circumstances such as economic downturns. They are less like to cut their expenses and to distinguish between making purchases they really need and those they would merely like to make, continuing to spend on the nice-to-have items as well as core necessities.

The right customers are also less price sensitive; price is never their only or even main consideration. Many businesses seem to simply target the broadest possible market rather than considering which customers are most likely to want and be able to pay for their products or services, thereby offering the best potential profit. A single cash-rich client is potentially a much bigger asset than a number of budget-limited customers. It's worthwhile spending more marketing money to acquire them and investing more in retaining them when they have become your customer.

Find out who has a strong, immediate and motivated need and desire to buy what you're offering – the normal criterion for your ideal client. They need to be the people who make the decision to buy, and whose decision is not driven by price alone.

Figure out how your goods or services can connect with the interests of these potential customers. Spend time in places where they spend time: more expensive shops, restaurants, clubs and so on. See this as an investment for your business, not an extravagance. If the kind of client you want to attract spends most of their time in shops like Harrods or Harvey Nichols, then there's no point in spending your time in a local supermarket. You have to go out and see what they see, do what they do, feel what they feel and think what they think, experiencing their journey and the way they live their lives. It's also important to read what these people read and watch what they watch. In other words, develop a comprehensive understanding of what makes them tick.

Research is key. Form focus groups and ask questions like "If you were to buy product A, what would be your considerations before buying?" What people do they know? Connect with the people who work with them, as a way in.

These customers may respond in higher numbers to recommendations and referrals from their network than more common-or-garden marketing methods, because they don't want to spend so much time on looking around or being messed about. Their time is precious.

Importantly, they may demand exclusivity. Look at Ferrari, for instance: they will bring out their top car and announce that only twenty or thirty of them will be manufactured – and price and sell them accordingly. Property developers building high-rise blocks may offer just one or two penthouse suites; they know that certain customers are attracted to the exclusively expensive; they want that special car or apartment or super-yacht. It's important to think about how you can make your product or service unique and therefore more valuable and more exclusive, so that people will want to purchase what you're offering.

Critically, see who else is selling to that market, and then look at their marketing to see what they're doing to attract such customers. Then adapt your methods accordingly, making them germane to what you're offering. You don't

need to reinvent the wheel, if somebody is already doing something successfully.

Action points

✱   Understand as much as you can about the habits of the more affluent customers you can target.

✱   Spend time in the places where these people are to be found.

✱   Work out how the goods or services you offer can appeal to those with more money.

✱   Think about how you can offer a degree of exclusivity to such clients.

3.4: THINK 'VALUE'

Key results you will gain from this section:

◊   *Why thinking 'value' is crucially important.*

◊   *Methods for adding value to your customer offering.*

◊   *Choosing the methods that are the most suitable for your business.*

Constantly think about how you can bring extra value to every customer for every pound they spend with you.

"How do I bring value and add value to this particular relationship?" This applies in every business relationship: with your customers, with your team members, with your suppliers, with your stakeholders, with your investors, with your bank manager, with your advisors – every relationship. And the more time you put into nurturing those relationships, the more you are going to get out of them.

Always think in terms of the most that you can give to a customer or client for every pound they spend with you, rather than the least you can get away with, which is

what very many businesses try to do. If you give them the maximum you can for their expenditure, they'll come back to you and spend more. My premise is that we get paid in line with the value that we deliver; the more value we deliver, the more we will get paid.

The ideal is to focus on making yourself so valuable that you become indispensable, that people need you and rely on you for whatever you offer. You can also add value not just directly through the product or service you offer, but by sharing your knowledge, experience and expertise. Best of all, sharing your network and contacts with people is always a winning strategy.

In my accountancy practice, we changed the business from helping clients with accountancy-based compliance and a number-crunching business, to an advisory business. We started asking ourselves what clients really care about: do they care about improving their business; do they care about working less hours and spending more time with their family; or do they care most about enhancing their profit margins? Then we asked ourselves, what can we do to add value in those areas, because those are the things that our clients ultimately want to achieve.

To add value, you can think about what else a customer in that sector wants that you can deliver, and that you don't currently offer. For instance, if you're a public speaker, in addition to your speech content you can give your audience tools that they can take away and use, perhaps follow-up material in the form of videos, or step-by-step guides. In the day nursery I run, we added after-school clubs and it proved very popular. As noted earlier, a cash and carry wholesaler client added storage units to his business so that his customers could buy in bulk; it was a gamechanger for him. Disney is constantly generating a host of add-on services – see under *Breakthrough Thinking* in section 3.6.

Action points

* The more value you deliver, the more income you will generate.

* Create value through indirect activities as well as through your commercial offering.

* Think about how you can expand the range of goods or services you currently offer in order to create more valuable offerings.

3.5: MARKETING METHODS THAT MATTER

Key results you will gain from this section:

◊ *A survey of marketing methods.*

◊ *The importance of choosing the right methods for your specific situation and objectives.*

◊ *The benefits of marketing differently to your competitors.*

There are many tools available to market your business, but the newest ones are not always the best.

My simple rule for marketing may surprise you; it's to observe what the majority are doing and then do the opposite. Marketing is not a 'dark art', a mystical process with secrets known only to the initiated. It's more a mixture of maths and behavioural science and understanding – and the emphasis is on the maths. It's all about the numbers.

Let's look at some of the best tools that are available out there for you to use in your marketing, and how to choose the methods that matter.

In the good old days of advertising-led marketing, the only platforms available were TV, radio and newspapers. All three were high cost, so you had to be a big company or have a big budget to market through those channels. But today you can have your own TV channel via YouTube and your own radio station using podcasting. You can have a daily broadcast using Twitter, and you can publish your own feature articles and press releases using LinkedIn or Facebook. The whole process by which we use marketing media has been transformed and keeps on transforming.

I believe that email marketing is overused, mainly because it's free; and because it's free, everyone wants to use it and so the customer is flooded with email offerings and may well ignore all of them (or have them directed automatically to their spam folder). Email marketing has its place, but more effective methods are available out there for small business owners to exploit; those channels mentioned above are the ones I believe you should definitely be exploring.

Of course, that doesn't mean you should ignore some of the tried, tested and trusted techniques. I believe direct mail is still an excellent way to accurately reach your potential customers and prospects, engaging with and speaking directly to them through your copy.

Giving talks and presentations is another brilliant way to get your message out there; it builds your credibility and your personal and business brand, and it puts you across as an expert. People are always looking for speakers. It's not easy

to secure speaking gigs, but I believe many more people should persevere and use speaking as a marketing tool.

Networking is another viable marketing method if you do it right. It tends to be a slow-burn process to build relationships before you start to get results, and you have to be networking in exactly the right circles. If you want to reach high value clients, you have to operate in high value networking circles. Try different networks to see what works best for you to get the right fit.

Some networks seem to function only as revenue raisers for those who start them. Many networks seem to contain a lot of professionals who haven't got a lot of work and so have time to be serial networkers, and they can be desperate to get work. In these circles there can often be many more sellers than buyers – hunters rather than farmers, as I call them – and there can be people who are very salesy, pressing their business card into everyone's palm. Successful networking needs to be a much more in-depth and empathic process than this.

Networking works particularly well for certain types of business, such as handymen, computer repairers, electricians or other tradespeople, because most professional people don't have them in their address books, and they can find potential customers in any group.

Referrals, however, are one of the most effective ways to market yourself in order to get more customers. Ask yourself, what am I doing on a daily basis to cultivate more referrals? How many times am I asking my customers for a referral? The answer, I find in most cases, is "Not enough!"

But in addition to asking clients, you should be thinking about which other suppliers in your particular market sector can be harnessed to refer clients to you. For instance, let's say you run an accountancy company; you should be thinking about building strong links with suppliers such as bank managers, financial advisers, solicitors and law firms – and you should be referring customers to them and getting them to refer customers to you. These reciprocal relationships steadily build strong and lasting links of mutual marketing benefit.

If you're operating in a niche marketplace, you can organise unique networking events for your customers, also inviting those other suppliers who operate in that specialised segment – in the example above, bank managers or IFAs or solicitors - so that they can meet your customers. You can also invite them to bring a few of their own customers. For instance, you might organise small evening meals for groups of eight to ten people, where you can have an informed chat together about the current trends in your shared market area. This is a very powerful marketing method for securing high value new clients.

You should also look at running your own seminars to attract large numbers of new clients. Webinars are a very cost-effective method of achieving the same results.

We have looked at a range of effective marketing options, from direct mail to YouTube, to Facebook, to podcasts and webinars. These are diverse assets, and the more marketing assets you have, the more leverage you can exert in your marketplace; and the more credibility and kudos you can build. In this way you can become a micro-celebrity in your specialised field. The more you can do this, the more people will talk about you and the more prospects you are going to attract to your business.

People talk about social media marketing. I hear a lot of entrepreneurs worrying and saying that they don't know how social media marketing works. I don't believe that social media is marketing in itself; it's a platform, just like speaking is a platform, a way to get your marketing message out there – a form of execution – and it's important to understand that distinction.

The key point to remember with anything you do in marketing, however, is this. People want to hear a story and want to be part of a journey. Every business entrepreneur should have a story running through their marketing, which will serve to distinguish them from all the others. People out there constantly want to connect with other people and have always done so. But nowadays – in a very 'noisy' world - making genuine connections is more crucial than it has ever been.

Action points:

* The more marketing assets you can exploit, the more leverage you can exert in the marketplace.

* Always make use of the free modern social media, but only use email marketing if you know for sure that it works for you.

* Consider using direct mail marketing.

* Have systems in place to constantly get referrals from customers and industry suppliers.

* Give talks or webinars and develop blogs to become a leading expert and micro-celebrity in your field of specialisation.

* Have a compelling story element running through all of your marketing measures.

CHAPTER 4

KEY THINKING ON FINANCE AND ACCOUNTING

CASE STUDY

———————o———————

Hassan Ali ran a large recycling business, moving recycled materials from those who needed to get rid of them to those who would pay to make use of them. Mike worked very hard and moved a lot of materials, yet he couldn't get his annual turnover above £200k. He had perpetual cash flow problems.

Hassan had experienced a tough upbringing in a deprived area. He lacked self-worth and ability in managing money: he was just uncomfortable with it. As a child he had always lived in an environment of financial shortage. He felt he had done quite well to even get where he was but suspected that he could do better if he could work out how and change the way he was doing things.

The simple fact was that Hassan was having perpetual cash flow problems because he was not charging enough for his services, which was because he had an aversion to charging higher. When he looked at his books more closely, Hassan realised that he had ongoing agreements with long-term clients where prices had not changed for years and were now extremely low. Examining his customer accounts individually, he realised that there was no consistency or methodology running through the customer base: a few clients showed a good margin of profit; a few more showed a small margin; a lot of clients were being charged at break-even point; and quite a number were creating a net loss.

Hassan decided he must bite the bullet and instigate a more consistent pricing system in which all customers were paying pro-rata the same fair price based on the service they were receiving, and the goods being

delivered. He assumed that by doing so he would lose most of the clients who had been paying lower prices for years, but this turned out not to be the case.

This key change worked extremely well. Profits immediately rose, and Hassan was reassured by the fact that all these clients appreciated what he was offering and stayed with him. Importantly, this started to trigger the desire for change in Hassan's mindset. He decided to go to a consultant who taught him about how money works, why understanding the numbers is so important in business, and how crucial financial discipline is. Mike also learned about the power of underlying beliefs and attitudes in being able to do all this. Over a period, he began to question his own long-held attitude that money is not a good thing and that making a healthy profit is not a 'bad' outcome. Over time he also realised that he had to value himself in order for others to value him. The penny dropped, and he began appreciating himself more. All this enabled him to further the pricing policies he had begun to put in place. The business's finances improved dramatically.

Considering his business model further, it dawned on Hassan that the biggest cost to his business had been acquiring the trucks he needed to move recycled materials from A to B. But these trucks were never in continuous use. Hassan hit on the idea of offering haulage services to other businesses in the locality. This was an immediate success and created a significant additional income stream which was highly profitable as the equipment had already been paid for.

Now that Hassan was generally charging more all round, profit increased, and cash flow was hugely improved. Thinking about what he had recently learned about money and how his attitude to it was evolving, he realised that he wanted to use any excess funds wisely. He got financial advice and began to invest in wealth accumulating assets which included buying property and stock exchange index funds. Not bad for someone who not so long ago had been completely uncomfortable with money!

Nonetheless, Hassan was still Hassan and he understood that there were limitations to his ability to manage advanced financial matters. So as the business grew, he began to bring in an accountant on a monthly basis to look at his management accounts and keep an eye on his cash flow, in particular the business's Key Performance Indicators. As performance grew still further, he hired an expert to come in once a week to give him a weekly picture of how the business was performing.

Hassan's annual turnover had now gone up from £200k to £10m. And in terms of his relationship with money, he was a different person altogether.

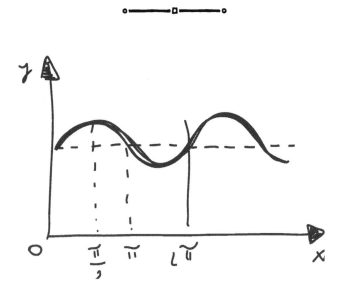

THE RECIPES

4.1: MONEY MINDSET

Key results you will gain from this section:

◊ *The connection between money mindset and personal traits.*

◊ *How to change your money mindset.*

◊ *Understanding patterns in the way money works.*

Changing your money mindset in order to do better business may involve challenging some of your habitual ways of dealing with and thinking about money.

People can have a problem with their self-worth. Somehow, they don't feel deserving, worthy or justified in securing further success than they're currently achieving. At an unconscious level this may be influenced by society's oft-presented depictions of money – 'Money is the root of all evil'; 'Money makes you a bad person'; 'We're only working here to pay the bills'; 'Money doesn't grow on trees'; 'Money changes you'; and so on.

But the real truth of the matter is that money is a good slave and a bad master. Money can amplify who you really are; if you're a good person it can make you an even better one, if you're a bad person it can turn you into a monster. You are in charge of your behaviour and your traits; that's not the fault of money. If you're unable to control and influence yourself when you have money that's not because of the money itself.

I hear a lot of people saying that more money equates to more problems. But think of it this way: right now, you might not have much money, but you will still have some problems – that's because everyone has problems. You might as well have money and problems rather than problems and no money. The money may even be useful in addressing some of the problems you have. Money can make many aspects of existence easier.

In reality, money is simply a means of exchange: nothing more, nothing less. Treat it as a servant and you'll be fine; but remember that money has no loyalty. Today it's yours but tomorrow it's someone else's. It is not something you should worship or fall in love with.

Money has certain traits. If you get to know what these are and behave accordingly, then it will move in your direction. That's because wealth generation is not about pursuing

money; it's about attraction, becoming a money magnet. Here are some of money's traits:

QUICK TIPS

- Money loves speed, those who move first have an advantage. I suggest that you avoid procrastination and start putting your ideas into action. Money creates lasting motivation and motivation creates momentum. What are you doing today to put your ideas into action?

- Money likes process. Look at process-driven businesses like McDonald's, Amazon and others; they are successful largely because they are dependent on process and not on people. Having a business that is dependent on systems and processes as opposed to people (who can be unpredictable and unreliable), will generate more money. Process helps you get consistency, gives your team members clarity, and enables things to be done according to the way you want to run your business. I find that the smaller the business, the more likely it is to be people-led. If this is you, do what you can to change this with systematically organised and written processes and checklists.

- What processes can you introduce or improve upon in your business to become more process driven, less people dependent and more profitable? For instance, have a well-defined, written down sales process so that anyone who joins your sales team can follow that process and sell in the way your business sells. If you have a customer service department or person in charge, have a very clear process for how you deal with customer complaints. And let's say you're a painting and decorating company, you can have a system for how you start a job, another for how the work is carried out and a third system for quality control and snagging on completion.

- Money likes courage. It is attracted to people who take calculated risks and are able to curtail postponement or procrastination – because tomorrow never comes. Those who are bold enough to make their dreams come true are the ones who succeed. If you were being truly courageous what would you do that you haven't done before?

Always value yourself and make sure that you pay yourself each month, on time. Lots of small business owners only take money if there's anything left in the pot; that's the wrong way to do it, because if you don't value yourself enough to take money out each month then why should others value you?

I suggest you have two or three different bank accounts. Have one for tax and VAT, another as a savings account (transferring money to it on a regular basis, only to be used on wealth-accumulating assets), and the main business account.

It's all about becoming comfortable with money. Although you can be in business for different reasons - which might include making a positive difference and creating a better world - you are still a business so you're there to make money and you shouldn't be embarrassed about that.

Keep an eye on how much money is owed to you by customers. I find that lots of small businesses I support run into cash flow problems because they don't chase up outstanding debts, or have trouble securing payments. In thinking about this matter, there is a motto commonly heard in business: 'Get money from customers quickly, pay suppliers slowly'; I disagree. I always try to pay my suppliers as soon as I can. It is a trait that goes with a good money mindset, and means you get your debts out of the way, so you know exactly where you stand financially. Furthermore, if you're prompt with payments your suppliers are more likely to give you bigger discounts, which helps improve your margins.

Action points

* Remember that money is a good slave and a bad master.

* Understanding and acting upon money's traits will enable you to attract it.

* Don't avoid taking money out of the business for your own needs.

* Use different accounts for different financial purposes in the business.

* Chase up outstanding debts meticulously.

4.2: GETTING YOUR PRICE RIGHT

Key results you will gain from this section:

◊   *Why pricing is your single most important decision.*

◊   *The effects of higher or lower pricing on your business performance.*

◊   *Practicalities of effecting price change.*

Pricing is the single biggest factor impacting on your business's bottom line, so you need to get it right.

A percentage increase in price has a much bigger corresponding percentage influence on profits. Don't be fooled by the common idea that a small price increase of say 2% to 3% is not going to make a significant improvement.

The buyer's perception is the key element in pricing, and the key point about perception as it affects pricing is this: in most business settings, people will pay you according to how they perceive your business offering and your business to be and - this is the crucial bit - based on their emotional response, feelings and perceptions.

Someone who goes to Harrods in London automatically expects to pay more than they would at a less well known or less prestigious retailer. This result has been achieved by Harrods in a number of ways, including:

- Their name and their brand.

- Where they are situated.

- Their history.

- The décor and layout in store.

- Their atmosphere and 'presence'.

- Their standard of quality.

- The esteem in which they are held.

This even extends to the bragging rights acquired by a customer simply by carrying a Harrods bag. Compare, for instance, the impression created by someone walking down the street with a supermarket carrier bag. The fundamental principle is this:

The way in which customers perceive you and your product, directly equates with how they perceive your pricing.

When will buyers be happy to pay more? If people see value in what you're selling, and if they see it as helping them achieve their desired personal or professional outcomes in life, then they will pay more for it. For instance, if you're an accountant who can improve a client's cash flow by saving them £20,000 in tax, then you can charge more than they were paying formerly. Even with an increased payment for services they will achieve their desired outcome – more income.

There's another important factor here – selling based on the value you provide. This works well if you know the monetary value of the outcome as you can charge a fixed percentage depending on how much you help someone make or save. Value pricing will not be covered here in any further depth as there are already plenty of books on that topic.

The principle is exactly the same for any business, with any product or service, in any industry. If you help people get what they want, they may be willing to pay more. For example, a smoker is spending on average £2,000 per year on cigarettes. If you can actually help them stop smoking at a charge of £500 – even if it's double what others are charging, but you have a product that works better – then smokers will pay your charge because they're still saving £1500 a year. The ways in which you might enhance your offering, helping assure customers that it meets their desired outcomes, are covered in more detail under the section 'Think value'.

Where many business owners go wrong is in failing to increase the price regularly. Some will increase their price every two or three years, or every five years; but the longer you leave it the bigger the increase you will need to implement. If you increase your price every four years and by a significant 10%, then customers may be upset because of the steep rise. But if you do it in increments of 2 or 2.5% every single year, for example, customers can accept that because they're aware of the reality of inflation and they know that your costs will be going up too. So small, steady increments are far better than occasional big hikes. And crucially, the cumulative positive effect on profits of a 2.5% rise every year for four years is bigger than that of 10% every four years.

However, I'd strongly suggest that you don't just increase your prices. You should also look at creating additional value alongside each price change. One strategy for doing this is providing package options of good/better/best or bronze/silver/gold standards for the client to choose from. By providing choice and different levels of service/product, the customer or client is more likely to find a solution that works for them, and you are not forcing them into a simple yes/no decision.

Another option for increasing your price is to give clients more certainty by offering a 100% money-back guarantee if they're not happy with the product or service. If you do this, you will be differentiating yourself from the marketplace and you can charge accordingly.

Action points

* Whatever you do, never under-price.

* Add value to your offering so that you can command higher prices.

* Think about the outcomes you can provide which will persuade customers to pay a higher price.

* Sell to customers who are less price sensitive.

4.3: CREATING MULTIPLE INCOME STREAMS

Key results you will gain from this section:

◊   *The dangers of having a single revenue stream.*

◊   *Why multiple income streams are disproportionately beneficial.*

◊   *Ways of adding extra income streams.*

Having a number of revenue streams is crucial to building a business's success and prosperity.

Far from being a positive, the number '1' is the most dangerous number in business: relying on just one customer, or one supplier, one employee, one type of marketing platform, or one form of technology, all are potentially dangerous for a business. Dangerous because when that one particular element becomes redundant or unavailable, having no alternative means your business will inevitably suffer.

And this applies all the more to having only one income stream. Things can so easily go wrong: something changing in the economy or in your sector, or new government regulations that cripple your one revenue source. Precisely

because of this I run five separate businesses; they're all very different and they have different customer types. Obviously, I'm not advocating that every entrepreneur or business immediately launches four additional interests, but the need for additional income streams is a vital one.

There are different ways that you can make sure you have multiple income streams. Firstly, you can add an extra stream to your existing business - something that compliments what you have already – or you could enter into a joint venture with a non-competing business. Think about what happens whenever you buy from Amazon - "Hey! Customers who bought this also bought that and they bought this other thing too!" Similarly, you can offer corresponding choices for your buying customers; or you can refer them to other businesses and earn commission that way.

Let's say, for instance, you're a website designer. When clients have a website designed, they will also want that site to have visibility, so you could either introduce them to an SEO expert or build this into your own service. Likewise, you could extend your service or get commission by introducing them to social media marketing, copywriting, blog provision, photography or video production. These are all good hand-in-glove fits for your core business.

Another way of building additional income streams is to offer an extended warranty to cover a product or service you already provide. The margins on these tend to be much higher than on the original purchase price. John Lewis does this very successfully; DFS do it on their furniture sales by offering cleaning kits with huge margins. What can you do that is low-cost to you with a high margin, and is a good fit with whatever the business already offers?

Another option is to invest in another business. I have helped a lot of clients do this to great effect. You may remember earlier we discussed the wholesaler who opened a range of storage units – it complimented the existing business but also built a new, separate income stream.

Look closely at the connections you can make with your own business venture. What ideas can you come up with for additional income streams?

Action points

* Add extra income streams to your existing business model.

* Add external options, such as entering into joint ventures.

* If relevant, add warranties or secondary products which have a higher margin than your main service.

* Invest in another business.

4.4: INVESTING IN WEALTH-ACCUMULATING ASSETS

Key results you will gain from this section:

◊ *Why wealth accumulating assets bring such great benefits.*

◊ *Different types of wealth accumulating assets.*

◊ *Which types are best?*

Investing in wealth accumulating assets (WAAs) is the surest way to increase your income and build financial security.

Money is more easily spent than earned. We're all pretty good at spending money when it comes in, but we're not always so good at earning it. There are always a lot of things that you can plan to spend your money on, long before you earn it.

The #1 rule in business, however, is to ensure you earn more than you spend. While the #1 thing to be avoided is making a loss. The #2 rule is to invest some of your profits so that money starts working for you as opposed to you working for money. Warren Buffet is the acknowledged world master at this which is why he is consistently in the top ten list of the world's richest people. You need to have this intention and you need to make it happen with action.

I personally always wanted to invest, but for years I put it off and spent my money on cars, holidays and clothes; but none of these things generate any cash. I needed some financial discipline. I opened up a savings account and started transferring a certain amount of my income every single month. That money was only to be spent on wealth accumulating assets - anything which in theory will go up in value and also generate income – such as property, stocks and shares, art or antiques. I find that property consistently gives a good return. Another option is buying another business or a share or partnership in one.

The compound effect of the increase in these assets over twenty years or so is going to be very significant, and that can then potentially become part of your retirement plan. It's important to start today so that you can build the biggest possible pot. If you do this over a twenty or twenty-five year period you're going to be able to retire earlier than most people who haven't been investing in WAAs. And over this period, you will not only have actual cash income, but some of these assets may well multiply in value over time – a double whammy of income plus more valuable capital assets. Other helpful things you can do include investing in pensions as well as government tax-free options such as ISAs.

Warren Buffet is the godfather of compound interest: read what he says about how it works here.[1]

But what if you think you are not earning enough or haven't got surplus income to do this? What I have found in my work with businesses is that more often than not people have problems due to the law of diminishing returns, usually because of spending more than is being earned.

But most businesses have the flexibility to decide that they are going to invest just 1% of their profits into a savings account, and then start building that up, a simple way to begin investing. Every business making a profit can afford to begin in this way and then grow in confidence as they start focusing on investing in other assets, gradually seeing 1% becoming 2% and then 4%. This isn't about 'can you afford it?'; it's 'can you afford not to do it?'

1. https://www.gurufocus.com/news/540137/warren-buffett-on-the-joys-of-compounding

Action points

* You have to make sure you earn more than you spend; investing some of your income in value accumulating assets is the best way to ensure this.

* Choose from such assets as stocks and shares, property, art or others listed above.

* Even if you don't feel you have much spare cash to invest, you can start in a very small way and then build up the investment over time.

4.5: FINANCIAL DISCIPLINE

Key results you will gain from this section:

◊ *Why financial discipline is essential.*

◊ *What to do if you are not good with numbers.*

◊ *Starting measures to create financial discipline.*

You cannot run a successful business without understanding and having a grip on the finances.

If I was given a pound or a dollar for every time a business owner said to me "I'm not good at numbers" or "I don't like maths" or "I don't understand the accounts" – well, then I wouldn't be writing this book, I'd be sitting in a sunny place with no internet, no mail, no phone and no bills to pay, enjoying my early retirement.

A lot of people are apprehensive or positively fearful of numbers, or at least don't make the effort to understand them – and I think that's a big shame. I would strongly recommend that you know the numbers in your business in order to build essential financial discipline.

I'm an accountant, but I didn't start a business in order to learn to sell – selling is not a priority in the accountancy profession, and the same goes for marketing, HR and customer services. But I learnt about all of them in order to have an understanding of how each of the different functions works in a business, in order to help my business do better. Nowadays I have others perform all these functions, but in the earlier days I had to learn them all for myself. Similarly, I believe that business owners need to grasp, understand and become comfortable with numbers for the benefit of their business.

One of the first things you should do is to make a twelve-month forecast and then you should stick to it. This should be part of your annual business plan; and there's no point in writing a business plan if you're not going to stick to it. Every single month you should review your management accounts and compare your actual performance against your planned budget. If you want to spend something extra outside that budget, then you need to justify that to yourself and your team members. If you're ever in doubt you should leave that expense out. The point of a budget is to know exactly where to allocate your financial resources in order to get the best return; it isn't there to curtail your spending, as many people think. A good habit is to first earn, then invest, then spend.

If you struggle with financial discipline, then a good place to start is to have separate bank accounts; then you can ask someone in your business, whom you trust, to look after all

the expenditure. Then employ a bookkeeper to do the day-to-day data entry. Many people in business don't put aside money for VAT or tax, so separate bank accounts can be set up for this and for other outgoings. Money put into these accounts can only be used to meet the type of expenditure they're set up for.

You also need to start looking at your accounts on a regular basis. Begin to understand your margins, different costs, and how they are related. I can assure you that among all the people I've worked with, coached, mentored or interviewed, the successful ones are those who have good financial discipline. There's a reason why among the FTSE top 100 companies there is a high percentage of CEOs who are accountants. It's the numbers that count, and it's important that as a small business owner you become comfortable with that.

Action points

∗ Overcome any aversion, diffidence or lack of interest you have in knowing your business's numbers.

∗ Make a twelve-month forecast and then stick to it.

∗ Every month, review your management accounts and compare your actual performance against your planned budget.

∗ Understand all the different financial components in your business, especially margins.

CHAPTER 5

CHANGING YOUR
MINDSET

CASE STUDY

———o———

Isabelle Noble was an ambitious general manager of a hotel chain with hotels in outer London and a number of UK cities. She had risen to the top of her industry through dedication and hard work, but in recent times found that they were struggling with lower occupancy rates and reduced income. She was doing things the way she had always been doing them, but now Isabelle began to realise that the times were radically changing for hotels - and she had not kept pace.

She was feeling frustration and a sense of unfairness that she should still be working so hard but not getting the results she wanted. She blamed the customers who had stopped booking with her chain and even felt resentment towards those customers who did book, as well as towards her staff around the UK.

Isabelle began to worry about losing her reputation or even her position, and this prompted her to take a long hard look at what she could do. It was time to stop doing things the way she had been doing them, and instigate some changes to reverse the negative pattern she was in. Isabelle knew she needed to think differently, so talked confidentially to some contacts she had in other hotel chains and came back with a to-do list.

Her first steps were intended to directly address the falling occupancy rates. Firstly, she initiated a system of staff bonuses to encourage better customer services and engage her teams in the process of reaching more customers and getting more bookings. This positively affected the atmosphere between herself and her colleagues around the chain,

changing relationships from mutual resentment to a win/win scenario. Then she introduced price incentives and loyalty points to encourage repeat bookings and referrals by customers, which created another win/win relationship. Occupancy rates steadily began to improve.

Next, Isabelle began to target a broader range of customer offerings to include conference facilities, accommodation for business meetings, networking events, and hot desks which small business owners and sole traders could rent by the week, as well as weddings and birthday parties. She engendered a working relationship with the business community around each of her city locations so that local business people thought of her hotels when they needed accommodation for visitors or associates.

These measures worked very well; but Isabelle now had the bit between her teeth and looked at how thinking differently could be carried still further. Her boldest step was to buy up a holiday park where vacationers and second homeowners could rent lodges, on the edge of a National Park. This was such a success that she bought up more such lodges around other National Parks, and this in due course became one of the key features for which her hotel chain became known.

Isabelle's position was now secure. And colleagues in the hotel business were now coming to her for confidential advice.

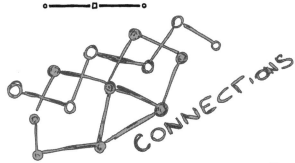

THE RECIPES

5.1: THINK WIN–WIN

Key results you will gain from this section:

◊ *How the win/win philosophy works.*

◊ *Overcoming aversion to letting the other party win.*

◊ *Practical applications of the win/win principle.*

Being successful is not about winning at the other person's expense.

When you're in business, it's obviously important to go for what you want, to look after yourself, and to look after your business – these are clearly part of your responsibility.

But in order to be genuinely successful – and to achieve that success more swiftly – you have to be thinking about the other people connected to your business, and saying to yourself, "Okay, what can we collectively do, so that

everyone benefits?" I'll give you a couple of examples which demonstrate the value of this principle.

Examples of win-win

If you have X number of staff, ask yourself: "Why are they working for me?" or "What do they ultimately want to gain from working for this business?" Then, if you support them in achieving what they want, they'll get more out of it – and you'll get more out of it too, to the benefit of the business.

In the simplest terms, if you say to your team: "My baseline target is to reach \$/£100k profit per year; so if we make that, I'll give you all a bonus; and if we make any further profit beyond that figure, we can share that extra revenue." It seems simple, but now your team is more aligned with you and your aims and prepared to work harder for you because they know they'll get more out of the business becoming more successful. It's win/win.

The same idea applies in negotiation. Rather than thinking about how you can screw the other party down to the last penny, you could say to them: "In this particular deal, what aspects are *really* important to you?" When they tell you, you can say, "If we can accommodate these things, then let me share with you what is most important to me." Now the negotiations can positively accommodate the priorities of both parties.

Don't be selfish and think just about yourself – think collectively, think as a team – whether with your clients or customers, your employees or colleagues, your investors or shareholders, or anyone else you're doing a deal with. Always think, "How can we *both* benefit?"

The commonest mistake here is not letting the other person also win. I was always taught that it's better to have 50% of something than 100% of nothing, and that has served me well over the years. Many people think that business is about being cut-throat and ruthless; it's not. It's more about saying: "How can everybody in this particular scenario benefit?"

When you start habitually thinking this way, adopting this attitude and using this kind of language and communication, then you'll find that you'll be doing more deals and you'll be making more money.

An entrepreneur client of mine sold his business for millions. He had received three offers – two of them about £10m higher than the third. He accepted the lowest offer. The reason was that it included keeping on current staff and making zero redundancies. Most observers would expect him to take the highest bid, but it was important to him that staff who had been working with him for many years would be looked after when he moved on. He was therefore willing to take less money; for him this was the win/win.

Often, someone commissioning a builder will most often go with the lowest quote, but other factors can also be taken into account, leading to a different choice. The customer may be willing to pay more, for instance, if the builder can guarantee that the work will be completed within a given timeframe. The client's win is the assurance that the work and disruption will be of a known and limited duration, while the builder's win is the higher price, enabling him/her to prioritise the job over other demands on the company's time and labour.

But most builders will still try to come in cheapest rather than thinking creatively about what else they can offer the customer to get the contract. Think about what the most important factor is for the other party, and then find a way to accommodate that.

Think creatively about it. Money isn't always the most important single factor to all parties in all situations; there are many other elements which some people may care about more in specific situations.

When taking on staff, I always ask interview candidates two questions:

1. Why do you want to work here?

2. What would be of most importance to you as an employee?

They may tell me, for instance, "I will take a £5k pay reduction if you give me a car." For other people, having a title and being known as a senior manager or an executive director is a central consideration for them and for their career trajectory.

We don't know what's important to any individual until we ask, and we can't make assumptions. Very often, it's something other than money.

It is about being mindful of what other people want when they're doing business with you, and then striving to ensure that you can accommodate them while still pursuing your own objectives. When you accommodate others, they will naturally accommodate you.

Action points

* When negotiating with other parties, always go in with three options – ideal, realistic and fallback.

* Always go through all the possible questions the other side might ask and prepare some great answers.

* Research first: know enough about the other side and how much they want the deal – this will help you negotiate.

* Work out your margins, to understand how much you can negotiate.

* Put yourself in the other party's shoes, and then think what you would do or offer – this will help you see things from both sides, so that everyone can win.

5.2: "THE WORLD IS UNFAIR!"

Key results you will gain from this section:

◊ *The dangers of apportioning blame.*

◊ *The importance of taking responsibility.*

◊ *Turning a problem situation into an advantage.*

Business is unfair at times, but there are things you can do about that, and become even more successful.

The world is an unfair place. Life is tough. People can be unforgiving. Get used to it; the quicker you can get over it the better. We're all in the same boat, facing similar challenges and similar struggles, overcoming similar obstacles and hurdles. We need to take responsibility and make the best of wherever we are right now.

I find that too many people are spending time apportioning blame onto others; it's never their fault, it's always somebody else's fault when something goes wrong. Even though that may in some cases be true, this is not a helpful attitude to take. The successful entrepreneur always takes responsibility for everything – good, bad or indifferent – and then says, "How can I do things next time in order to avoid being in this particular unwelcome situation?" This is a functional rather than dysfunctional attitude, and an effective rather than ineffective strategy. It's all about "What can I do about it?" rather than "Why is this happening to me, and why is life so unfair? Why are people so bad?" In business you must be a grown-up, not an adolescent.

Taking responsibility requires focus, and in order to be focused you need to take control so that you can improve your situation. The bottom line is that you don't want to be a BMW: in this case, an acronym for people who bitch, moan and whinge about other people. You can do this all you like, but no-one is going to come and sort things out for you. You've got to take responsibility for where you are and accept that you are where you are due to choices you made or circumstances beyond your control. And in order to avoid being in a similar situation next time, you've got to make different choices.

A client of mine bought a piece of land and was advised by the selling agent that she would be able to get planning permission for development on the land. After she had made the purchase, she instructed an architect and a planning consultant to plan a development, which was a major outlay for her. She was then told that she needed a variety of other reports to go alongside a planning application, which she commissioned. She eventually put the planning application in, but permission was refused. She ended up £75k out of pocket - in addition to the purchase price of around £100k - and with a piece of land that was next to worthless.

My client could have sat there and blamed the agent and blamed the architect and the other consultants; but she didn't do that. She acknowledged that this was a significant mistake. She should have done her own research, checking with due diligence before purchasing the plot. She should have gone into the deal with her eyes open and scrutinised everything in depth every step of the way.

She could have let the unfortunate aspects of this deal hold her back; but she held onto the land, moved on, and carried out other property deals. A few years later she revisited the project, reapplied for planning permission, and was able to build a number of flats there.

The experience could have been a terminal business experience for many people who might think that being several hundred thousand pounds down was the end for them and that life would never be the same again. Others would have sued the parties who had given bad advice and spend a lot more money on that. My client buried such thoughts. She took responsibility for everything that went wrong, learnt from it, moved on, did other deals, came back later, and made it work.

You win some, you lose some

No-one wins all the time. Losing is valuable in business because it teaches the most effective lessons – not necessarily at the time, but certainly when we look back later. Tom Watson, founder of IBM, said: "If you want to be

successful, double your rate of failure. Make those mistakes and make them quicker."

In retrospect, you may realise that the low points were the ones that took you to the high points. You learn more from your low points and your losses than you do from your successes. Furthermore, you can only enjoy the high points once you have experienced the low ones; otherwise you have nothing to compare them with. It's only when times are bad and then subsequently improve that you're able to enjoy the good moments; therefore, it's important to not allow losses and failures to hold you back.

Action points

* The business world is unfair. Get over it.

* Accept responsibility for everything that happens to you.

* Keep thinking "How can I change things next time in order to avoid being in this particular unwelcome situation?"

* Remember to learn as much from your low points and your losses as you do from your successes.

5.3: BE BOLD AND THINK DIFFERENTLY

Key results you will gain from this section:

◊　　　*Identify particular ways in which you can be more effectively daring in your business decisions.*

◊　　　*Discover that trying new things can be the way towards much greater success.*

◊　　　*Consider those ideas that may seem a little too unconventional to take a risk on.*

It's not a good idea to spend too much of your time being overly apprehensive or reserved about the business decisions you're making.

I meet very many people who have expertise and experience but lack the courage to make the **right** business decisions. What creates this inertia? It's the fear of failure. People can spend far too long overanalysing what to do and what might happen; this leads to a kind of fear-based paralysis. It's much better to pursue your dreams and put in the graft till you get what you're after.

I would like to encourage you to go out there and get what you want in life and in business – to be who you really

are – because you deserve it. Don't be a backseat driver in your own business; don't sit on the fence when making decisions.

When you think of something you want to do, or something you want to achieve, have confidence in going ahead and doing it. I'm not advocating recklessness; but sometimes you have to set fear aside and just do it – have the courage to get on, stop beating about the bush, and get things done. So – as long as there aren't clear and strong reasons not to - go ahead with those expansion plans, or bring in that new product line your customers are calling for, or take on more staff to support a department that is currently too stretched to produce at full capacity.

We all enjoy being in our comfort zone, but in business a simple desire for straightforward linearity can inhibit progress. As an entrepreneur you must be open to things being different, otherwise there will be no growth, either personally or commercially.

People so often don't take that next step - the one that would make the big difference - and get on with pursuing their goals. It can be because they're overly cautious or overly laid back; or perhaps they're not motivated enough, or simply not prepared to take the risk. But a lot of the time business is about taking risks and just getting on with it.

QUICK TIPS

- Try a new line of business.

- Come up with a new product.

- Package an existing product in a different way.

- Hire a manager who can do things you're not good at presently.

- Solve a known problem in a quite different way from what you've tried already.

Fear of failure

I've found that one of the biggest factors at play is fear of failing or of making mistakes. There's usually a causative factor at work. Perhaps they've made a mistake and been burnt in the past, and now they see the same potential scenario coming up, and they don't want to go down that road again. Or maybe they've just been brought up to view failure as the ultimate disaster and are always going to be overly cautious and risk averse. Whatever the origins, these people have stopped innovating and testing out new ideas, or implementing new strategies, which will stultify their business.

You need a reasonable layer of protection, of course, but in business you really do need to be brave. It's very often

through failure that success comes. Most people don't fail by trying things out – it's actually the other way round: **if you fail to try, you'll never be successful**. Failing to try is trying to fail. And crucially, you can learn valuable lessons from any failures and then apply that learning in order to be more successful.

When businesses stop trying things out, look at what can happen to them:

- Blockbuster video retail chain thought Netflix et al would never catch on – and went bust. Worse than that, Blockbuster's CEO passed up the chance to buy Netflix for a mere $50m – it's now worth more than $100b[2]

- Toys "R" Us didn't invest enough in the online business, and went bust[3]

- Maplin relied too much on opening new walk-in stores, and they too went bust[4]

---

2. https://www.businessinsider.com/blockbuster-ceo-passed-up-chance-to-buy-netflix-for-50-million-2015-7?op=1&r=US&IR=T

3. https://www.news.com.au/finance/business/retail/the-real-reason-toys-r-us-went-bust/news-story/6f5c0fcf51ae5de220d282ed815b2f3f

4. https://hackaday.com/2018/03/01/bye-bye-maplin/

QUICK TIPS ✅

- Develop your ideas.

- Be brave.

- Try stuff out.

- Get on with it.

- Be gutsy. What is there to lose, ultimately?

It's the crazy ones who change the world

Another aspect of the benefits of being bold in business can be found in Steve Job's motto, "*Those who are crazy enough to think they can change the world usually do.*" Your best ideas – the ones that change your business or even the world – may be the most unlikely ones.

Here's what I think: starting a business is one of the craziest things you can do, because you end up being employed by a lunatic: that lunatic is you. Think about it; why would someone work extra hours, take less holidays, take a pay cut, take on more worries and stress, and so on? Only a mad person would do that. So welcome to the world of business! You've already done one of the craziest things ever, so why not continue on that path, and achieve bigger and better things?

What I find is that we are quick to limit ourselves, with limiting thoughts and beliefs which hold us back, like "That is not going to work" or "I've tried that before" or "This thing hasn't worked for other people." But we've got to have the mindset to do what nobody else has done before, so that we get what nobody else has achieved before. To do that, we must be disruptive enough to do things in a very different way.

'Think Different' is the well-known Apple slogan, used in their adverts for a number of years, and it's applicable to every entrepreneur. One of the key questions I get my clients to ask themselves is "What can I do today in my business that's going to change the world and make it a better place?" That means having a paradigm shift, thinking outside the box, challenging yourself to be different.

This disruptive strategy not only directed Apple's innovations such as the iPod, iPhone and iPad – innovations which then became the industry standard - but is evident in many other influential cases.

Ben & Jerry's made the first ice cream that had big lumps in it; no-one had ever done that before. Rivals argued that it would never sell. But it became a distinguishing characteristic of the product, and one of the key reasons customers bought it; other brands had to start putting lumps in their ice cream. The reason they did it in the first place was because Ben Cohen had no mouth taste, only 'mouth feel'.[5]

Bob Newhart agreed to recording and selling his comedic material. Many told that it was a bad idea and that people would stop coming to his shows as they would get all they needed from listening to the jokes. The opposite happened; *more* people started attending his shows as a result of listening to his audio material.

People thought a bagless vacuum cleaner would not work. Dyson made it work before anyone else. See the interview with Dyson in *Inspirational Gamechangers*, by Gerry Maguire Thompson, Financial Times Publishing, 2016.

Who would have predicted that Facebook would work as successfully as it has? It certainly didn't sound like a good idea in the early days; it looked like it would never take off. Yet now it boasts billions of users.

---

5. Interview with Ben Cohen: included in "Inspirational Gamechangers", by Gerry Maguire Thompson, Financial Times Publishing 2016

What disruptive ideas can you come up with, that make business sense? Here are some examples of steps you might take along these lines:

Action points

✱ Be 'crazy' enough to do things in a very different way.

✱ Be open to a paradigm shift, thinking outside the box, challenging yourself to be different.

✱ Don't allow yourself to be held back by limiting thoughts and beliefs that you may come from your past.

5.4: GIVE IT ALL YOU'VE GOT

Key results you will gain from this section:

◊   *Identify personal patterns of holding back.*

◊   *Sports people as examples of the principle of giving it all you've got.*

◊   *Apply the principles sports people use, in a business context.*

Don't hold back or you may regret it later.

Having worked with a range of entrepreneurs and other businesspeople over the last 17 years, I've often observed that people in business express regrets. And one of the most common refrains is "I wish I had done X, Y or Z," regretting not having tried harder, or tried to do more things than they have done.

Being successful, using whatever definition one may wish to apply, is primarily about showing up and performing. Mo Farrah, for example, is someone I personally admire very much; he certainly gives it everything he's got. But the same applies to almost any of the outstandingly successful individuals you can name in sports, such as Michael Jordan in basketball, or Jessica Ennis the heptathlete.

These sportspeople demonstrate the kind of commitment we need to show in business. It's obvious to me that top professionals in the sports arena do that more comprehensively and consistently than entrepreneurs in business. Of course, all of us have good and bad days, but the mindset we need to develop is that we must perform like a true professional, like our sporting heroes, every day in business. Research these people and see how they behave, how they think, how they train, how they look after their mind and body. All of these things will help you give 100% every single time you show up.

In business, this could mean asking yourself what you can do to train yourself and develop the skills most relevant to yourself such as speaking, writing, selling, marketing, time management, management or leadership.

Top athletes also look at the power of incrementally making small marginal gains in as many areas as possible – looking at every specific factor in their performance. This is precisely how the Sky cycling team came to dominate world cycling competitions under the regime of Dave Brailsford. We can do this too in our businesses, looking comprehensively at everything about the business and then working on aspects that are under-performing or showing up as a weakness. Small marginal gains in multiple areas add up to disproportionate greater gain overall, in much the same way as compound interest works.

Top athletes also take particular care of their overall health and wellbeing. In my view entrepreneurs should do so too, because it affects your business as well as yourself. In my experience a large number of professionals neglect this, and can suffer from diminished performance or even burnout.

Finally, all leading sportspeople have a coach or mentor who teaches their speciality. I recommend you do this too.

The way I like to do it is to think that if today were my last day, how would I perform? That is how I tackle every single day. When someone asks me, "What is the best day that you've had so far?" I always feel that the best day is yet to come. If I've already had my best day, that means that I can't do any better; and I always think that today or tomorrow could be my best day. Being better with each new day should be the aim.

In order to give the best you've got, you have to have clear focus. You've got to have a positive attitude and mindset. You've got to be optimistic. You've got to look after your health. When I've studied people who are exceptionally successful in the business arena, I find that they all emphasise the importance of living a healthy lifestyle, including some form of regular physical activity or sport. In my case, this observation led me to engage a personal trainer and make time for focused exercise, and I've also managed what and how much I eat. The impact of these steps on my energy, fitness, discipline and clarity of

thinking have been a gamechanger for me, and greatly helped me in my business success. These are all valuable transferable assets which you can use in business.

The habit of holding back on making the maximum effort can be the result of past failures or negative experiences or be due to a lack of confidence. The sporting analogy again applies here. Successful sporting figures do not let these things hold them back but overcome them by creating new positive experiences to replace the undesirable ones and persisting so that confidence is built up again. The more you practice, the better you'll get.

So if you've had a product that didn't do well, or a decision that turned out badly, look at that and think, this is a gift to me: what can I learn from it, so as to move forward and improve? Look towards the future because it is the only part that you can affect and change.

It's important, too, to have a mindset that the more we give, without expectation of reward, the more we get in return, in any area of life. In business, the more you give to your clients, the more you will get back, whether directly from them or indirectly from others. I seek to give 100% to everyone I interact with, in every single conversation, during every single meeting. You should do the same, not forgetting that you will have bad days – that's part of life. It's how we deal with issues on the bad days that define us.

You should leave no stone unturned in your business efforts and ventures, so that you won't end up with regrets, telling yourself you wish you had done this or that. Instead, why not do it now, so you can say that you always showed up and you always gave it the best you had.

Learn from others' mistakes

The one thing I have done consistently in my life and career – and probably the only thing I've done consistently – is making mistakes. Some of these could quite easily have been avoided – especially the really costly ones. The way to avoid mistakes is to look and listen; observe what others do, learn from them, and avoid the costly mistakes you see others make.

There are many examples of mistakes made by large and otherwise successful companies, and they provide lessons that we can all learn from. Kodak, for instance, disastrously failed to recognise the onset of digital photography until very far into its development.[6] Blackberry came up with the first smartphone and led the market for a while, but failed to evolve and wasn't able to develop the technology as Apple did. A young person today won't even recognise the Blackberry brand.

------

6. https://www.forbes.com/sites/chunkamui/2012/01/18/how-kodak-failed/

Action points

* Have a clear focus on what you want to achieve.

* Have a positive attitude and mindset.

* Be optimistic.

* Don't let past failures hold you back.

CHAPTER 6

CHANGING YOUR
PERSONAL
THINKING

CASE STUDY

Mindi Patel sold insurance in New York, working on commission for one of the big international insurers.

Mindi had started out positively on this career path and had done well on the commission system, but at a certain point, after a difficult family experience, she entered into a somewhat despondent phase. This adversely affected her work, as she was taking a rather negative feeling into meetings with potential corporate customers, and found she was not now converting so many leads into sales. The personal change also affected her sense of how people were responding to her. She wanted to make a good impression and be liked so that she could make more sales, and went out of her way to be extra nice to potential customers, but this often came across as being desperate and put many clients off. Sometimes she was making promises she couldn't later deliver on, in order to gain favour.

At home, she found herself dwelling on her misfortunes, regretting missed opportunities in the past, and fretting about the future. Her work/life balance wasn't great either; she seemed to be working more hours but getting less results, becoming stressed, and not taking any time off for hobbies or fresh air and exercise – something she had always prioritised in the past.

On a holiday in Greece - which Mindi had booked the previous year - she attended a course in yoga and meditation. She enjoyed the course and had time to reflect on where she might be going wrong and what she could do about it. Away from her habitual preoccupations and the stresses of work situation, she realised that the key was going to be letting go of her emotional baggage and learning how to live less in the past and future and more in the present. On holiday in the sun, she was able to practice this – enjoying the moment, as it is.

Mindi returned from holiday determined to take a serious look at herself and her more negative tendencies and patterns. Something she had learned on the retreat was to think about experiences less in terms of mistakes and more in terms of opportunity. She decided to go to work each day with the attitude, "What is the most that I can achieve today?"

She also instituted a personal regime where she made sure to take proper time for rest, restarted jogging which she had stopped for a while, and started allowing herself to watch box sets at the weekend. In fact, she viewed the eight seasons of Games of Thrones over four consecutive weekends, marching into work on each of the following Monday mornings with fierce and optimistic determination to close deals – which she started to do once more.

Customers noticed the change in her and responded positively. This in turn helped her mood. After a while she noticed that she hadn't thought about whether she was the flavour of the month for some time; yet people seemed to be holding her in higher esteem and passing on glowing feedback from clients. Respectability, it seemed, was more important to clients than likeability: down-to-earth straightforwardness and an honestly good deal, combined with a reputation for doing things on time and as promised.

Mindi was back in the groove.

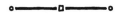

6.1: LIVE IN THE MOMENT

Key results you will gain from this section:

◊ *The problem with dwelling on the past.*

◊ *How to think about the future without distracting from the now.*

◊ *Benefits of living in the present.*

The ability to live in the present moment is essential for the greatest business success.

In life we all make mistakes, and most of us make mistakes on a regular basis; but we should not allow those mistakes to hold us back. In fact, we should see each mistake as an opportunity to consider what we can learn from a particular experience, and what lessons we can take going forward.

That is a good way to view mistakes. Unfortunately, what I often see in my work is people holding onto those mistakes forever, never wanting to try again whatever was being tried out when that happened. This can severely limit the confidence to try anything new at all. Because people have made those mistakes, they are continuously living in the past, always dwelling upon what happened two or five or ten years ago. This can lead to missing what's right in front of you, what's happening in the moment. It's important to let go of that 'excess baggage' as I call it, because it's not good for your mindset, for your decision making. Move on from the past – you can't change it. It's important to let go, free yourself and move on. When you do that, you're going to be able to operate at a totally different level, because you can be more in the moment, living in the now.

It's equally important to not overly worry or dwell on the future. How many times have you worried about something potentially happening in the future, only to find things turned out very differently?

Of course, as we noted, it's key to have a plan of where you want to go and what you want your business to look like, but there is no value in having a spreadsheet of hundreds of different potential scenarios and outcomes, then worrying about every single one. Instead, like Mindi, think "What is the most that I can achieve today?" That thinking will enable you to operate at a much more effective level, and help you be a lot more focused, a lot more disciplined. Only then will you be addressing the key factors that are influencing your business and your life right now.

The present is the only place where achievements can be made. You can only juggle so many balls at once so it's important to focus on key priorities.

The past is for learning from, not for living in. You don't want to reside in the past, because it never enables you to move on.

Action points

✳ Focus on what's right in front of you, what's happening in the moment.

✳ See each mistake as an opportunity to consider what you can learn from that experience, to take forward positively.

✳ Don't overly worry or dwell on the future.

✳ Constantly think "What is the most that I can achieve today?"

6.2: WORK/LIFE BALANCE IS KEY

Key results you will gain from this section:

◊ *The effects of overwork.*

◊ *The dangers of burnout.*

There's a reason why they talk about Work, Rest and Play.

I own five businesses and do quite a bit of other work too. I'm a city councillor and work as a board director and as a trustee for a number of charities. People who know me think that I am a workaholic; I love work, I love getting stuff done. But what I've learned the hard way is that an overworked brain is not a productive brain. Just because you're working twelve, fourteen or sixteen hours a day doesn't mean you're achieving more. Better to work fewer hours but make every hour count.

It's important that you take rest, because your body and your mind need rest – that's the way we're built. There is plenty of research showing that workplace productivity is dropping significantly, because people are overworked and stressed.

It's a bit like a test match in cricket. You're there for five days; so you have to pace it out. If you think you're going to win that match in two or three days, it's not going to happen that often. If you're a batsman, you're going to take risks in your innings, miss shots and get out. If you're a bowler, you're going to push yourself too hard in the first four or five bowling overs, you're going to be burnt out, and then you're not going to be able to put in those extra six or seven overs. In other words, in either case, you're not going to be able to change the game.

It's all about taking it easy and understanding that you don't have to graft like mad in order to get results. There's a very good reason why the tortoise beat the hare in Aesop's oft-cited fable. The tortoise had a balanced judgement of the race and the journey, while the hare went like crazy, misjudged the timing and then didn't last till the end, thereby losing the race. There's a lot of wisdom for business people in that particular story.

Action points

❋ Take enough rest.

❋ Do activities that enable you to switch off.

❋ Remember that you don't have to graft like mad 24/7 in order to achieve results.

6.3: LIKEABILITY VERSUS RESPECT

Key results you will gain from this section:

◊   *The dangers of striving to be liked.*

◊   *The key to winning respect.*

Once people respect you, they may well end up liking you as well.

I've spent a lot of time in business wanting to be liked. But at a certain point in my life it dawned on me that wanting something and having it are two very different things. I decided to give up on being eager or desperate to be liked by other people and was surprised to discover that from that point onwards more people liked me. I believe the key factor is that it's better to be doing things which earn us respect rather than things we believe will make people like us.

Respect usually lasts longer than likeability. In the process of worrying less about whether you're likeable, you might sometimes upset people, because someone may not like a particular aspect of the way you go about your business; but at least you are being true to yourself. You could do 100 good things for someone, but the odd occasion when

you let them down will be the day that they will always remember. They'll soon forget the 100 good things you did. It's an advantage if people respect you for being principled and true to who you are, and how you do things.

Likeability is highly subjective and depends on personal preference, usually based on how that person feels at a given moment. It changes with situations and circumstances, and with emotional changes in the liker/ disliker. You could be the dish of the day one moment, yesterday's flavour the next. Why aspire to gain something that's not in your control? Whereas, once people respect you, over time some of them at least will end up liking you as well.

You need to have the ability to make difficult decisions by always being objective. You won't please all of the people all of the time, so why try to do that? Do what you do best, in the way that you do it best, and through that you will gain respect. And people will probably like you too!

Action points

✳   Don't focus on being Flavour of the Month.

✳   Do things that gain you respect rather than things that you hope will make people like you.

✳   Consider what people will think about you in the long term rather than short term.

CHAPTER 7

LEARNING FROM COVID: RISK AND CRISIS MANAGEMENT

Key results you will gain from this section:

◊　　*Develop a systematic approach to risk and crisis management.*

◊　　*Assess possible risks to your business.*

◊　　*Put systems in place to deal with risks that could materialise.*

Never wait until you're in a crisis to develop your crisis management plan.

At the time of writing in May 2020 the coronavirus pandemic and measures for its control are dictating business activity. Few of us, if any, could have foreseen this, and the economic effects have been so dramatic that it is difficult to imagine what steps could have been taken if we had. So let's use this as a prompt, and an opportunity to learn generic lessons in order to prepare ourselves and our businesses for whatever may happen in the future.

That's what business risk assessment is all about: identifying the possible risks and the impact on your business if they happen. Crisis management is the implementation of steps to combat or alleviate the consequences. Resiliency will be greatly increased by anticipating risks and preparing for dealing with them should they occur.

An example of a risk assessment chart is given at the end of this chapter.

"That's Never Going to Happen!"

Many events become crises because they arrive when people are unprepared for them. There is a common tendency to think a whole range of things are never going to happen. These often later become 'famous last words'.

Business risk assessment is all about taking account of the unthinkable, the disaster that seems unlikely – as well as of course the more usual everyday business risks. There are two questions to ask yourself. The first is 'How likely is this to happen?' and the second is 'What would be the impact on the business if it did?'

Let's look at a couple of examples.

It's quite likely that your telephone system or internet could go down for half a day, and the impact of this would depend on the type of business you are running. If you run a mini-market with a huge footfall, it may be nothing more than an inconvenience, but if you run a business mainly dependent on telephone and online purchases it will make quite a dent in your takings. Not only will customers be unable to contact you on that occasion, but they may look for an alternative supplier and be lost to you forever. This not only applies to your existing customers, but you'll never know how many potential customers you've lost because they couldn't contact you.

The first principle to take on board is that a comprehensive business risk assessment will consider all the risks that you think could possibly affect your business, however unlikely some of these may be. Of course, if you recognise a risk where no amount of planning will overcome the effects, then there probably isn't any point in including it in your risk assessment. I'd say that these risks are very much the exception. In most cases you will be able to work out some strategy to meet - or at least offset - the effects of a risk actually happening.

With those first principles in mind, let's move on to how you might draw up a business risk assessment together with a strategy for crisis management. Anyone with a responsibility for Health & Safety in the workplace will probably recognise some of the tools and strategies.

This is hardly surprising as the aim is exactly the same - identifying the risks and managing them to an acceptable level. Think of it as health and safety for the business itself.

Identifying risks

Essentially there are two types of business risk - those you can't control and those you can.

Looking at the first type, there are two mnemonics that you'll find helpful here, both used in business analysis. The first of these is:

S	Strengths
W	Weaknesses
O	Opportunities
T	Threats

Let's assume a business is very heavily dependent upon the expertise of its founder and let's also suppose that the founder is reluctant to delegate, or to mentor and support employees who could ultimately take over some of the founder's business functions. It's a common enough situation, especially in businesses that depend upon professional or technical expertise or a creative instinct. It's rare to find good business management skills in the same person who has the driving creativity or expertise.

So the inherent weakness in that business model is the over-dependence on one person. What is going to happen if that person is suddenly removed from the business by death, ill-health or accident? A further issue is that the person in question may steadfastly refuse to recognise that this is a weakness in the structure and that poses an ongoing problem for his or her colleagues. That's a problem that can be identified but not necessarily solved by a business risk assessment, but the identification will at least flag up for the potential successors that they themselves need to formulate a strategy for when the time comes, even if they can't implement it yet.

With regard to threats, the second mnemonic classifies the type of threat:

P   Political

E   Environmental

S   Social

T   Technological

How much of a threat these are to any particular business really depends upon what that business does. For example, a business that has developed a technological solution may be threatened by new technological developments. A

business selling a product which is not considered 'green' will be threatened by the ever-growing environmentally-conscious lobby.

The thing to always bear in mind, though, is that what appears to be a threat can just as easily be an opportunity. The firm which has already made technological advances can embrace and carry forward the new technology to its advantage. The business selling products that don't meet current environmental standards may be able to modify or diversify.

Some analysts add categories like Legal and Ethical and come up with a mnemonic such as PESTLE. The 'Social' category also includes Cultural and Demographic, and could be referred to as 'Socio-Cultural-Demographic'.

However you choose to remember them, these threats are **macro-environmental**. They relate to conditions which affect the economy as a whole, not just a specific region or sector. This includes things like gross domestic product (GDP), inflation, employment, spending, and the monetary and fiscal policy.

All of the above risks are outside your control.

Alternatively, the threat may not be macro-environmental in the true sense of the word, but it may affect either the whole of the sector in which you operate; or it may affect your immediate business environment. This could be a change in standard product specification, new regulations, or a change in the regulatory regime for businesses which provide a service. These are **micro-environmental** threats and there's a mnemonic for these factors too:

C	Competitors
O	Organisation Itself
S	Suppliers
M	Markets
I	Intermediaries
C	Customers

As you can see, you may be able to exert a degree of control over some of these, for example issues that arise within your own organisational arrangement. However, essentially you will be **reacting** to them (however much advance planning is involved).

Finally there are the risks that are specific to your business, and in many cases you will be able to manage these **pro-actively**. For example, a key employee might be

head-hunted. What could you do to manage this risk? You have two different types of solutions.

The first is to make it difficult for the employee to leave. You could try imposing restrictions such as covenants against working elsewhere, but these seem to be less enforceable than they once were, and you can only enforce them through court action.

How much better to use the carrot rather than the stick and use strategies such as favourable working conditions, performance-related pay, employee participation in business profits, peer recognition etc. That's what I call a proactive approach.

Your business risks will fall into one of three categories as follows:

TYPE	AREA AFFECTED	CONTROL	APPROACH
Macro-environmental	Global or national	None	Reactive
Micro-environmental	Region or sector	Some	Reactive
Business-specific	Just your business	Near-total	Proactive

When I refer to a risk being 'business-specific' I don't mean that it is a risk that applies to your business alone and to no other business. There are risks (and other factors) which occur in all, or nearly all, businesses, but the way in which they affect your business (and how you may be able to deal with them) is specific to the individual business.

So every business will have its own particular risks but some that are common include:

- Loss of suppliers.

- Shrinking of target market, owing to shifts in customer requirements.

- Competition, from a technically superior product, or a new competitor business.

- Changes in legislation or public policy, for example, no smoking rules if you're a tobacconist.

- Changes in product specifications or regulations.

- Lack of government funding if you're a not-for-profit organisation.

- Change of fashion. Do you still sell the 'must-have' product?

- Failure of equipment.

- Shortage of or sub-standard raw materials.

- Widespread sickness absence.

- Breakdown in employee relations leading to industrial action.

- Loss of personnel.

- Shortage of appropriately qualified personnel or other recruitment issues.

- Loss of reputation.

- Economic downturn and global or national financial forces.

- Changes in political climate.

- Environmentally conscious factors such as climate change, reduction of CO_2 emissions.

- World or national events e.g. war, epidemics, environmental disasters.

I urge you to think outside the box and ask yourself the questions: 'Why do my customers buy from me?' and 'What could happen that would make them stop buying from me?' It's practically impossible for one person to think of every possible risk. This really is a case where team input can produce a more comprehensive result.

What you have to do is try to imagine all the possible scenarios that might happen (and which might have nothing to do with your trading model). I don't suppose very many people will have had a business risk analysis that took into account a complete lockdown, as was the case with the COVID-19 outbreak.

Finally, although I've pointed out that you are **reacting** to macro-environmental and micro-environmental risks, a successful business risk assessment and crisis management strategy will always adopt a **proactive** approach to identification, measurement and management. If you wait for the risk to happen, it's almost certainly too late to manage it effectively.

How do you measure risk?

By now you should have a good idea of how to go about identifying the possible risks. This is only the first step. The next thing you have to do is to measure the likelihood of it happening. As I mentioned at the beginning of this section, some things are much more likely to happen than others!

My suggestion is that you grade the likelihood of each risk happening. You can use 'Low/Medium/High' or 1 to 5, or whatever system you prefer.

Of course you are making something of a guesstimate. I've outlined above the distinction between the three types of risk - those that you can control, those where you have a degree of control and those you can't control at all. Which category a risk falls into doesn't matter for the purposes of measurement. The only risks you can completely ignore for the purpose of the business risk assessment are those where the impact would be so momentous that you would be concerned only with the physical survival of yourself and your family.

Take your list of identified business risks and for each one, consider as objectively as possible how likely this is to happen. Don't underestimate, but don't overestimate either. Clearly, if any event is on your list, you've admitted that there is at least a possibility that it could happen (otherwise you wouldn't have put it on the list in the first place). So each and every risk will have a value, and if you think it's extremely unlikely to happen then that value will be the lowest category i.e. 'Low' or '1' depending upon which system of classification you're using.

So hopefully you've now got a list of all the risks and you've worked out how likely each of them is to happen. You've still not finished with the measurement side.

Now, for each risk, imagine it has happened and work out how it would impact on your business. Let's look at some examples:

- You are suddenly and dramatically undercut on price by a competitor.

- A technological development makes one of your key products out of date.

- Strike or other industrial action either in your business or in the supply or delivery chain.

- Theft of products or cash by an employee and the insurance won't pay up.

- Breach of customer confidentiality, complaints or other events resulting in damage to reputation.

- Inability to access premises, for example because of fire, flood or a crime scene.

- Customers fail to pay your invoices.

All of the above would have an impact on your business in the short-term or in the longer term. Your next task is to work out, irrespective or what you intend to do about it, what that impact would be. Depending upon your business and on the nature of the risk, you may want to analyse the impact for the short-term, medium-term and long-term.

Try to quantify the potential impact. Once you've done this, you should be able to plot the following:

A. Risks with a high likelihood of happening and a high impact if they happen.

B. Risks with a high likelihood of happening but a low impact if they happen.

C. Risks with a low likelihood of happening but a high impact if they happen.

D. Risks with a low likelihood of happening and a low impact if they happen.

Insurance Issues

We'll now move on to the next stage, which is where you give some thought to the measures you're going to put in place to reduce the level of impact.

If the risk exists at all, then in most cases you're not going to be able to do much to reduce the chances of it happening, especially where the risk is macro-environmental. You've already assessed the likelihood of this by the classification that you've assigned to it. What we are now doing is looking at ways to maintain the risk at its present level of classification (or, if possible, reduce it) and which indicate the crisis management steps already in place.

Before we do so, let's have a look at the way in which insurance can assist. In theory, with the exception of fraud, dishonesty or other criminal acts on the part of the insured person or organisation, it's possible to insure against any event. It's a matter of cost and of course of finding someone to underwrite the risk. In practice, the cost may be prohibitive, or it may prove very difficult to obtain cover, for many different reasons.

You may find that some of the risks you've identified are not covered, either because of the unavailability of cover or because of the cost. In these cases, the decision not to insure has already been taken. What about the risks that you can insure against?

It's far too easy to have a false sense of security about insurance. Not all insurance policies are created equal. You may think that's rather an obvious thing to say, but when was the last time that you looked at the terms and conditions of your policy in any detail?

There are two points to watch out for and these are 'Exclusions' and 'Definitions'. Exclusions are fairly easy to spot as the Schedule to your policy will usually list these. Do also have a look at the general terms and conditions however as there may be some exclusions there which apply to all policies, or which apply unless they are specifically referred to on the Schedule.

When it comes to Definitions, you'll usually find these in the Definitions section of the general terms and conditions, but there may also be definitions on the Schedule or in some cases in different parts of the terms and conditions. The key point here is not to make any assumptions. Generally speaking, the definition as set out in the policy document is the one that matters, not your version of what it should mean!

Let's look at an example from the Covid-19 situation. The majority of businesses have suffered an interruption in their business activities as a result of the COVID-19 pandemic. A good many of them have insurance cover for business interruption. So, you'd think there was no problem in making a claim, but in a large majority of cases you'd be wrong.

According to the Association of British Insurers, what most businesses have is standard commercial insurance which provides cover against a wide range of day-to-day risks including damage caused by fire and flood, theft and accidents involving employees. Very few such policies include cover against business disruption caused by notifiable or infectious diseases, and, even if extension cover has been purchased, it is likely to be restricted to specified diseases, not to diseases that may emerge at a later date. A further problem is that the cover may apply only where the disease is present on the business premises.

One of the reasons for businesses finding that they lack cover, is that the average business will have been sold a 'standard' package. This is not necessarily a criticism of the way in which insurance is sold, but a reflection of the economic fact that insurance is expensive. In addition, very few people read their insurance policies in detail (or if they do, they only do it once and it is surprising what tricks the memory can play. There's also the fact that it's very difficult to envisage all the risks that might come into play but let's hope this chapter is helping you with that!

Apart from standard commercial insurance cover you can purchase a specific disaster recovery policy. The cost of this is likely to reflect the vulnerability of your business and of course the measures you have in place to protect against risk and to manage a crisis should it arise. Your Business Risk Assessment should help you if you decide on this route.

Let's move on to the measures you might consider in order to mitigate the impact of business risks, bearing in mind that insurance is only one aspect of these.

Risk Mitigation and Disaster Recovery

Are there any steps you could take to ensure that the level of risk doesn't escalate? Where the risks are day-to-day ones that any business might encounter, such as a loss of customers as a result of dissatisfaction, or theft of business cash or property, then the steps to be taken will be those consistent with good business management, such as a robust and timely complaints-handling procedure and security measures surrounding the handling of cash and stock.

You may feel that issues of this type come under the heading of good business management, rather than crisis management, and this is true. However, the point of including them in your business risk assessment is firstly to create a complete picture, and secondly because these kinds of incidents, if unchecked, can very quickly amount to a crisis with a significant impact on the business.

Turning to the sort of events that most of us think of as a crisis, these include:

- Long-term unplanned absence of managing director or key director/manager.

- Loss of key personnel.

- Damage to premises making them (temporarily) unusable e.g. fire.

- Major local disaster (e.g. widespread flooding) or extremely inclement weather.

- Loss of utilities.

- Loss of telephone/internet services.

- Loss of IT services generally.

All of these are events which have the potential to cripple a business. The key is to ask yourself the following three questions:

1. If it happened, how long could the business survive without serious losses?

2. What could we do if it did happen?

3. What steps can we take now to minimise the chance of it happening and be ready to manage the crisis if it did happen?

This really is a case where forward-planning can save the business.

With regards to the absence of the director or key manager, the only real answer is to ensure that his or her functions are shadowed by someone else who can step in as necessary (easier said than done!). Key Man insurance cover (yes, this exists) would at least enable you to buy in some expertise.

Retaining the services of key personnel is really down to employee relations and incentives. Again, Key Man cover may provide a limited solution.

With the other scenarios, to some extent the impact depends upon the business, which is why the first question is so important. A large business trading entirely online will find the loss of IT services devastating, even for a few hours. Whereas a high street retail outlet will be unable to trade as usual if its premises are inaccessible, but, given availability of stock and alternative premises, will probably not lose out significantly.

There are no answers that meet the case for all businesses. What you are looking for is a solution that suits your business requirements, enabling the business to go on trading as smoothly as possible, and that can be implemented quickly with minimal disruption and at an acceptable cost. That's quite a challenge, but you also need to factor in the costs of not having a plan in place.

What you're looking for are measures that you already have in place, and which you feel mitigate the risk and the impact, together with measures that you can put in place immediately. In some cases, you may feel that the impact will be different in the short, medium and long terms. You can either note these differences in the measures column or create separate columns for each.

Then look at future measures that you can't put in place immediately, either because of cost or because they will take time to implement, such as training someone to shadow a role. Put these down in the next column. You don't have to have something written down in every column, but you should have something under measures for every risk. If you haven't it means that you have no strategy in place to manage that risk and none planned.

What's the next step?

Implementation and Review

You've identified your business risks, measured the impact, worked out what measures you already have in place and those that you're going to put in place, either immediately or in the future. So, what now?

I think it's a very good idea to have a column indicating whose responsibility it is to see that the agreed measures and plans are implemented and of course to monitor their effectiveness. This may depend on the size of the organisation.

The final column is the Review. It's really important that you regard this as a working document and one which is reviewed regularly. It's a good idea to set down how often the review should take place and this may be different for different risks. You can if you wish also use this column for the details of responsibility.

Date the document to when it was finalised, mark the date when the first review should take place and, moving forward, include the date of every review that's taken place as well as the date of the next planned review. That way you'll have a rolling record of the process.

CRISIS MANAGEMENT

I've given you a lot of information about how to assess your risks and how to plan for the impact, and this last section is about what to do when the crisis hits. If you've carried out the steps outlined above and kept your Business Risk Assessment up to date (and implemented the decisions), then you should have a blueprint to manage the crisis. Here are my top tips, should you find yourself in that situation:

TOP TIPS

1. Don't panic - you've done all your preparation.

2. Nothing is more important than the safety of yourself and your workforce - a point to remember if the crisis involves danger.

3. Let your workforce know at the earliest opportunity that there is a crisis management/disaster recovery plan in place.

4. Assign the appropriate tasks to personnel (if your plan doesn't already do this) so that everyone knows what they need to be doing.

5. Don't necessarily think you've got to do everything yourself.

6. Keep in touch with your staff with regular updates to let them know what's happening.

7. If unwelcome decisions have to be made, such as redundancies, don't put off telling the people involved. Uncertainty will make things worse.

8. Remember that whilst it is your business that is at risk, your workforce will have their own concerns, so be sympathetic to these.

9. Keep looking for other solutions and if there is any good news, then share it. It's good for morale.

10. When it's all over, learn from what happened.

Action points

*   Don't be tempted to write off potentially catastrophic but unlikely events as "That will never happen."

*   Identify all the risks, and then classify them as set out above.

*   Measure the respective likelihood of each of these risks happening.

*   Work out what the effect each of these risks might have on business.

*   Consider the measures you can put in place to mitigate the effects of these eventualities.

*   Make plans for implementation and review.

*   If a crisis happens, follow the top tips listed on page 191

EXAMPLE BUSINESS RISK ASSESSMENT REGISTER

Risk Likelihood/Impact

1 = Very Low   2 = Low   3 = Medium   4 = High   5 = Very High

RISK	LIKELIHOOD	IMPACT	EXISTING MEASURES	POSSIBLE FUTURE MEASURES	REVIEW FREQUENCY
Death or enforced unplanned retirement of managing director/sole director	2	5	Arrangement for qualified alternative manager to step in	Lasting Power of Attorney, testamentary arrangements	Annually, or in light of health
Long-term unplanned absence of managing director/sole director	2	4	Under-studying of management role	Private health insurance. Key man cover	Annually, or in light of circumstances
Loss of key personnel	3	4	Good remuneration package & working conditions. Incentivised remuneration. Hands-on management opportunities	Regular reviews between managing director and team members	Annually, or as outcome of appraisal
Damage to premises making them (temporarily) unusable e.g. fire	2	4	Robust fire and security precautions. Insurance including business interruption cover. Availability of working from home or from alternative premises	Purchase disaster recovery package	Six-monthly
Loss of access to premises (e.g. crime scene	1	4	Availability of working from home or from alternative premises	Purchase disaster recovery package	Six-monthly
Major local disaster (e.g. widespread flooding) or extremely inclement weather	1	5	Insurance including business interruption cover. Availability of working from home or from alternative premises	Purchase disaster recovery package	Six-monthly
Loss of utilities	3	3	Insurance. Availability of working from home	Purchase disaster recovery package	Six-monthly
Loss of telephone/internet services	3	4	Insurance. Availability of working from home	Purchase disaster recovery package	Six-monthly

EXAMPLE BUSINESS RISK ASSESSMENT REGISTER
Risk Likelihood/Impact

1 = Very Low   2 = Low   3 = Medium   4 = High   5 = Very High

RISK	LIKELIHOOD	IMPACT	EXISTING MEASURES	POSSIBLE FUTURE MEASURES	REVIEW FREQUENCY
Loss of IT services generally	2	5	Robust off-site ICT back-up. Use of cloud ICT system. Insurance	Purchase disaster recovery package	Six-monthly
Theft of records or equipment	1	4	Robust security arrangements. Inventory. Whistleblowing policy.		Three-monthly
Diminution of customer base generally	2	5	Monitoring and review on monthly basis in order to address issues as they arise.	Devise customer attraction and retention strategies	Monthly
Loss of customers as a result of dissatisfaction with service	2	5	Monitoring and review in order to address issues as they arise (customer feedback and satisfaction surveys).	Increase opportunities for customer feedback	Monthly
Loss of customers as a result of dissatisfaction with service	1	5	Open and transparent pricing. From advance quotations (service/professional businesses)	Benchmarking against competitor fees. Consider low-cost 'add-ons'	Monthly
Diminution of need for services as result of adverse economic climate	3	5	General economic situation kept under review as it applies to customers	Further observational systems interactive with customers to assist in pinpointing downward trends and 'danger-points'	Three-monthly
Loss of income as a result of unpaid invoices (service/professional businesses)	1	3	Payment of deposit or in advance. Ongoing work requires customers to pay by regular standing order. Terms and conditions of business provide for work to cease if standing order is not met.		Constant review
Loss of reputation	1	5	Detailed and robust office systems. Ongoing training to meet individual learning needs as identified through weekly 1-to-1 supervision and regular team meetings. Regular review for potential service improvement. Team involvement		Monthly

RISK	LIKELIHOOD	IMPACT	EXISTING MEASURES	POSSIBLE FUTURE MEASURES	REVIEW FREQUENCY
Professional negligence or product liability claims	1	4	Good office systemisation and training. Quality review system, Indemnity cover.		Three-monthly
Breach of customer confidentiality	1	5	Robust confidentiality agreements		Six-monthly
Theft of funds/assets	1	3	Robust financial security arrangements, including restricted signatures on bank mandate. Whistleblowing policy. Insurance. Inventory		Monthly
Theft of customers' money or other assets	1	3	Customers' funds are not held.	Should it be necessary to hold customers' funds in the future, consider a separate customer account with robust financial security arrangements and insurance cover.	If required
Damage to customers' property (services businesses)	1	3	Work not carried out at customers' premises	Insurance where work carried out at customers' premises or on their property.	
Occurrence of money-laundering offences (resulting in legal or regulatory action)	2	4	Robust money-laundering policy and procedures in place. All team members undergo training in dealing with ID checks etc and in vigilance as regards transactions		Three-monthly
Breach of professional regulations or industry regulations.	1	3	Ongoing training and review and regular update of understanding of regulations		Six-monthly
Falsification of records	1	4	Regular and random monitoring for accuracy		Monthly

EXAMPLE BUSINESS RISK ASSESSMENT REGISTER

Risk Likelihood/Impact

1 = Very Low   2 = Low   3 = Medium   4 = High   5 = Very High

RISK	LIKELIHOOD	IMPACT	EXISTING MEASURES	POSSIBLE FUTURE MEASURES	REVIEW FREQUENCY
Poor budgeting	1	4	Use of management accountancy to set budgets and plot actuals against budgets		Monthly
Absence of key skills	2	4	Cross-training to avoid over-reliance on individual staff members. Consultants and sub-contractors available. Good relationships with other professionals (where appropriate).		Six-monthly
Lack of business direction and growth	2	4	Mentoring of Managing Director who in turn mentors team members.		Six-monthly
Staff sickness/injury (or other staff absence)	1	3	Sufficient training for other team members to provide interim cover. Cross-training to avoid over-reliance on individual staff members Consultants and sub-contractors available		Six-monthly
Failure of Health & Safety measures	1	3	Robust H & S policy and regularly updated risk assessments	Health & Safety training	Six-monthly
Personal injury claims	1	2	Robust H & S policy and regularly updated risk assessments. Insurance		Six-monthly
HR issues/Employment Tribunal claims	1	2	Explicit employment contracts and policies/procedures. Regular appraisals and one-to-ones		Six-Monthly

First Approved on: Next Review Date: Last Reviewed on:

Business Risk Matrix   3 + = High

← Increasing Likelihood

A High Impact /High Likelihood	B High Impact /Low Likelihood
• Diminution of need for services - adverse economic climate • Loss of key personnel • Loss of telephone/internet • Loss of utilities	• Death or unplanned retirement of MD • Loss of IT services generally • Diminution of customer base generally • Loss of customers - dissatisfaction with service • Major local disaster • Loss of customers - dissatisfaction with price • Loss of reputation • Breach of customer confidentiality • Long-term unplanned absence of MD • Damage to premises • Occurrence of money-laundering offences • Absence of key skills • Lack of business direction and growth • Loss of access to premises • Theft of records or equipment • Falsification of records • Poor budgeting • Loss of income through unpaid invoices • Theft of funds/assets • Theft or damage to customers' money/assets • Breach of professional industry regulations • Staff sickness/injury/other absence • Failure of health and safety measures
C Low Impact/ High Likelihood	D Low Impact/ Low Likelihood
• Personal injury claims • HR issues/Employment Tribunal claims	• Personal injury claims • HR issues/Employment Tribunal claims

Increasing Impact →

CHAPTER 8

OVERVIEW: WHERE
TO FROM HERE?
NEXT ACTIONS

This chapter pulls together the key actions and tips from the rest of the book, to give an overview of vital behaviours, and to suggest where to go next to continue your development as an entrepreneur and business person.

You may wish to glance through the contents of this section, identifying the broad issues you most urgently need to address (e.g. strategy and business direction), then pinpoint the more specific issues you need to move forward on (e.g. growing your business) and you will find a short list of the key actions that will really make a difference to you and your business. I would advise making a separate note of these actions and devising an actual timetable for putting them into practice. Bite the bullet and do it now!

KEY ACTIONS AND NEXT STEPS, FOR KEY BUSINESS ISSUES

1: STRATEGY & BUSINESS DIRECTION

NO POINT IN RUNNING TOWARDS NOTHING

- Think through and write down: why you started your business, or why you are starting it now; what your priorities are in creating the business; what you want to gain from the business; and where you would like it to be in five years' time and ten years' time.

- Apply these principles as you build your business, or apply changes based on them if your business is already going.

- Remember these principles and continue to apply them as your business develops.

- Periodically review the business over the years, to check whether you are maintaining the priorities you set out at the beginning.

- It's possible that you may wish to change some of your priorities as progress. In which case, create a formally revised set of priorities, rather than just letting the original version slip, or having no priorities at all.

IT'S NEVER TOO LATE TO MAKE A START

- Take action now rather than procrastinating.

- Whatever has happened in the past is a source of learning for what you do next.

- Learn from people who have failed in the past and gone on to great success.

- Don't spend time comparing yourself unfavourably with others.

NICHING

- Have a look at your business offering and think about how making it more niche could help you do better.

- Look at your current client base and see if you have a sizeable number of customers in one area – make that your niche.

- Ensure your niche is a sector where clients are able to pay high fees – it must be a profitable niche.

- Ensure clients have growth mindset in that niche.

- Make sure you are passionate about that sector/ area.

- Do plenty of research to understand the sector if you don't know enough about it.

- Learn the language of the niche – each sector has different words and phrases which you must know in order to be part of the inner-circle.

COMPETITION: GOOD, BAD – OR BOTH?

- See competition as healthy and embrace it.

- Know who your main competitors are, and what they're doing.

- Only imitate what your competition is doing if it's a smart – and profitable – move for your company.

- Don't be fixated on your competitor's every move.

- Find clear ways of distinguishing yourself and your offering from your competition.

GROWING YOUR BUSINESS

- Use the classic core principles of business growth: correct pricing; more customer leads; ensuring customers buy more, more often; and that they stay with you longer.

- Systematise every process you can.

- Assess growth progress with key performance indicators.

- Diversify.

BREAKTHROUGH THINKING

- Look at how major entrepreneurs have made world-changing breakthroughs.

- Open-mindedly consider many potential solutions to a problem, then go with the one that brings a radically different approach.

- Take a break or change your location in order to get a different perspective on things.

- Come up with variations on what you're already doing to create new business opportunities.

- Aim high - be radical.

SUCCESS IS WHERE YOU LEAST EXPECT IT

- Don't just do what you've always done. Try out different approaches and see which ones work.

- Think strategically. Take a bird's-eye view of your situation and potential.

- Don't be afraid to do something different from your competitors in the marketplace.

2: CUSTOMERS AND MARKETING

KNOWING YOUR IDEAL CUSTOMER

- Do **not** believe that everyone can be your customer.

- Build a detailed profile of every aspect of your ideal customer: their demographics and their psychographics.

- Learn how your ideal customer talks and communicates and use the same language to connect with them.

- Work out where your ideal customer is to be found and connect with them there.

GENERATING LEADS

- Be very clear what kind of customer you want to be a viable lead for you.

- Use a variety of methods for generating leads and find out which work best.

- Using referrals is the single most powerful and cost-efficient method you can use.

- Work out the value to you of a lead, and from that work out how much you can spend to generate each new lead.

- Make sure each lead-generating activity includes a clear offer.

TARGETING PROFITABLE CUSTOMERS

- Understand as much as you can about the habits of the more affluent customers you can target.

- Spend time in the places where these people are to be found.

- Work out how the goods or services you offer can appeal to those with more money.

- Think about how you can offer a degree of exclusivity to such clients.

THINK 'VALUE'

- The more value you deliver, the more income you will generate.

- Create value through indirect activities as well as through your commercial offering.

- Think about how you can expand the range of goods or services you currently offer in order to create more valuable offerings.

MARKETING METHODS THAT MATTER

- The more marketing assets you can exploit, the more leverage you can exert in the marketplace.

- Always make use of social media. It's free after all! But only use email marketing if you know for sure that it works for you.

- Consider using direct mail marketing.

- Have systems in place to constantly get referrals from customers and industry suppliers.

- Give talks or webinars and develop blogs to become a leading expert and micro-celebrity in your field of specialisation.

- Have a compelling story element running through all of your marketing measures.

3: FINANCE AND ACCOUNTING

MONEY MINDSET

- Remember that money is a good slave and a bad master.

- Understanding and acting upon money's traits will enable you to attract it.

- Don't scrimp on taking money out of the business for your own needs.

- Use different accounts for different financial purposes in the business.

- Chase up outstanding debts meticulously.

GETTING YOUR PRICE RIGHT

- Whatever you do, don't under-price.

- Add value to your offering so that you can command higher pricing.

- Think about the outcomes you can provide which will persuade customers to pay a higher price.

- Sell to customers who are less price sensitive.

CREATING MULTIPLE INCOME STREAMS

- Add extra income streams to your existing business model.

- Add external options such as entering into joint ventures.

- If relevant, add warranties or secondary products which have a higher margin than your main service.

- Invest in another business.

INVESTING IN WEALTH-ACCUMULATING ASSETS

- You have to make sure you earn more than you spend; investing some of your income in value accumulating assets is the best way to ensure this.

- Choose from such assets as stocks and shares, property, art, etc.

- Even if you don't feel you have much spare cash to invest, you can start in a very small way and then build up the investment over time.

FINANCIAL DISCIPLINE

- Overcome any aversion, diffidence or lack of interest you have in knowing your business's numbers.

- Make a twelve-month forecast and then stick to it.

- Every month, review your management accounts and compare your actual performance against your planned budget.

- Understand all the different financial components in your business, especially margins.

4: CHANGING YOUR MINDSET

THINK WIN-WIN

- When negotiating with other parties, always go in with three options – ideal, realistic and fallback.

- Always go through all the possible questions the other side might ask and prepare some great answers.

- Research first: know enough about the other side and how much they want the deal – this will help you negotiate.

"THE WORLD IS UNFAIR!"

- The business world is unfair. Get over it.

- Accept responsibility for everything that happens to you.

- Keep thinking "How can I do things next time in order to avoid being in this particularly unwelcome situation?"

- Remember to learn as much from your low points and your losses as you do from your successes.

BE BOLD AND THINK DIFFERENTLY

- Be 'crazy' enough to do things in a very different way.

- Be open to a paradigm shift, thinking outside the box, challenging yourself to be different.

- Don't allow yourself to be held back by limiting thoughts and beliefs that you may come from your past.

GIVE IT ALL YOU'VE GOT

- Have a clear focus on what you want to achieve.

- Have a positive attitude and mindset.

- Be optimistic.

- Don't let past failures hold you back.

5: YOUR PERSONAL THINKING

LIVE IN THE MOMENT

- Focus on what's right in front of you, what's happening in the moment.

- See each mistake as an opportunity to consider what you can learn from that particular experience, to take forward.

- Don't overly worry or dwell on the future.

- Constantly think "What is the most that I can achieve today?"

WORK/LIFE BALANCE IS KEY

- Take enough rest.

- Do activities that enable you to switch off.

- Remember that you don't have to graft like mad in order to achieve results.

LIKEABILITY VERSUS RESPECT

- Don't worry about being Flavour of the Month.

- Do things that gain you respect rather than things that you hope may make people like you.

- Think about what people will think about you in the long term rather than short term.

6: LEARNING FROM COVID: RISK AND CRISIS MANAGEMENT

 TOP TIPS

1. Don't panic - you've done all your preparation.

2. Nothing is more important than the safety of yourself and your workforce - a point to remember if the crisis involves danger.

3. Let your workforce know at the earliest opportunity that there is a crisis management/disaster recovery plan in place.

4. Assign the appropriate tasks to personnel (if your plan doesn't already do this) so that everyone knows what they should be doing.

5. Don't necessarily think you've got to do everything yourself.

6. Keep in touch with your staff with regular updates to let them know what's happening.

7. If unwelcome decisions have to be made, such as possible redundancies, don't put off telling the people involved. Uncertainty will make things worse.

8. Remember that whilst it is your business that is at risk, your workforce will have their own concerns, so be sympathetic to these.

9. Keep looking for other solutions and if there is any good news, then share it. It's good for morale.

10. When it's all over, learn from what happened.

Action points

✳ Don't be tempted to write off potentially catastrophic but unlikely events as "That will never happen."

✳ Identify all the risks, and then classify them as set out above.

✳ Measure the respective likelihood of each of these risks happening.

✳ Work out what the effect each of these risks might entail to your business.

✳ Consider the measures you can put in place to mitigate the effects of these eventualities.

✳ Make plans for implementation and review.

✳ If a crisis happens, follow the top tips listed above.

Action is the catalyst for results. The best intentions and ideas in the world are inconsequential unless someone does something with them. You have invested time and money in your business. You have also invested time in reading this book. I want you to achieve remarkable results as a direct consequence. And achieve the success you deserve.

I hope this book has contributed to your thinking and given you helpful and useful action points to take you forward to business success, growth, and profitability.

Good luck!

HELPFUL LINKS

Here are some web and other resources which you may find helpful:

Start Your Business magazine

http://www.startyourbusinessmag.com

Federation of Small Businesses UK

http://fsb.org.uk

UK government resources for small businesses

http://gov.uk/browse/business

Simply Business

http://www.simplybusiness.co.uk

Entrepreneur Europe

http://www.entrepreneur.com

European Small Business Resources

http://www.ezilon.com/business/small_business

Small Business Association USA

http://www.sba.gov

ACKNOWLEDGEMENTS

It is a challenge to list all the people who support an author. This is not because there are not enough people; quite the opposite, because writing a book is a team effort - even though the author becomes the recipient of the credit and praise. The peril is that inevitably and inadvertently, some names get missed.

Therefore, I shall tread with caution and will do my best to broadly acknowledge all those who helped. My sincere apologies if I miss someone. I will have to make it up somehow; perhaps by writing another book.

First and foremost, I must thank my team at work. They help and enable me to create time to do the things I enjoy best. Thinking of new ideas and writing books are two of these.

Second - and most important by far - my family; they have always supported me. My wife Anila is extremely patient, considerate and caring. We have a young family and she ensures that everyone is looked after while I burn the midnight oil, cultivating new ideas.

Third, my clients. I have learnt so much from them. They inspire me every single day. Without them I would not have a business, let alone five businesses. They deserve my sincere thanks, and I am forever grateful to them for having put their trust in me.

Fourth, my literary agent, Susan Mears. She helped me find a brilliant publisher. With that I would also like to acknowledge and thank my publishers. They have been an absolute joy to work with; they made every step easy, enjoyable, and effortless.

Fifth, my long-time friend and editor, Gerry Maguire Thompson. He not only helps give the book added value but also challenges me to come up with clear thoughts and ideas. He always helps me create a better and stronger book.

I also want to thank all those people who have influenced me: writers, speakers, thought leaders, mentors, coaches and endless list of friends and associates of whom there are way too many to list here. You know who you are.

Shaz Nawaz, July 2020

"Shaz is interested in all aspects of business, and is the most well read and up-to-date person I know when it comes to business practice."

Austin Bambrook

Shaz Nawaz BA MA ACA, also known as The Profits Wizard, is a business consultant and author who runs five successful businesses of his own. Shaz has conducted over three thousand one-to-one business growth consultations to individual business owners and led thousands of businesses to greater growth and profit, in all sectors. This has given him a unique perspective on the challenges facing today's businesses and led to the development of his exciting debut title, *The Entrepreneur's Cookbook.*

Shaz's input has added over GBP200m in extra profits to his clients' businesses and raised over GBP150m in business funding and investment.

He is based in Peterborough, UK.

If you'd like to **contact Shaz**:

please email **shaz@aa-accountants.co.uk**

head to the YouTube channel: **Shaz Nawaz**

visit **http://www.aa-accountants.co.uk**

or use Twitter **@ShazNawaz1.**